Racial Justice

Racial Justice

Black Judges and Defendants in an Urban Trial Court

Thomas M. Uhlman
University of Missouri-St. Louis

Lexington Books
D.C. Heath and Company
Lexington, Massachusetts
Toronto

Library of Congress Cataloging in Publication Data

Uhlman, Thomas M.
  Racial justice.

  Includes bibliographical references and index.
  1. Criminal justice, Administration of—United States. 2. Afro-American criminals. 3. Afro-American lawyers. 4. Afro-American judges. I. Title.
KF9223.U35   345'.73'05   78-19569
ISBN 0-669-02625-5

Copyright © 1979 by D.C. Heath and Company

All rights reserved. No part of this publication may be reproduced or transmitted in any form or by any means, electronic or mechanical, including photocopy, recording, or any information storage or retrieval system, without permission in writing from the publisher.

Published simultaneously in Canada.

Printed in the United States of America.

International Standard Book Number: 0-669-02625-5

Library of Congress Catalog Card Number: 78-19569

To Beth

Contents

	List of Figures	ix
	List of Tables	xi
	Preface	xiii
	Acknowledgments	xv
Chapter 1	**Race and the Legal Process**	1
	Black Legal and Judicial Underrepresentation	2
	Race from the Defendant's Perspective	12
	A Study of Race in the U.S. Legal Process	15
Chapter 2	**Metro City, Its Court, and the Trial Court Data**	27
	Metro City–Demographics and Politics	27
	Crime and the Court	30
	Trial Court Data	36
Chapter 3	**Exceptional Achievements: The Background Characteristics of the Black Bench**	45
	The Black Bar in Metro City	46
	Localism–Birthplace, Childhood, Education	47
	Education–College and Law School Attendance	49
	Prejudicial Careers–Prosecutorial Experience, Government Employment, Private Practice	51
	Prejudicial Careers–Political Involvement	53
	Professional and Community Activities	55
	Method of Judicial Selection	56
	Conclusions	57
Chapter 4	**Indistinguishable Performance: The Decisionmaking of Black Judges**	63
	Measuring the Decisions of Black Judges	64
	Judicial Determinations of Guilt	65
	Sentencing Behavior	69
	Black Judicial Decisionmaking: Some Implications	72

Chapter 5	**The Defendant's Perspective: Conviction and Sentencing of Black Defendants**	77
	Interracial Disparities—Absolute Differences	78
	Interpreting Interracial Disparities—A General Path Model	82
	Interpreting Interracial Disparities—A Path Analytic Approach	86
	Conclusions	94
Chapter 6	**Where Do We Go From Here?**	101
	Appendix A	111
	Appendix B	113
	Index	115
	About the Author	121

List of Figures

5-1	Criminality Component	83
5-2	Class/Status Component	84
5-3	Racism Component	86
5-4	General Race-Disposition Model	86
5-5	Race-Disposition Model Including SES and Prior Record	87
5-6	Race-Disposition Model where SES and Prior Record Remain Unmeasured	88
5-7	A Fully Defined Race-Sentencing Path Model	89
5-8	A Reduced Race-Sentencing Path Model	92
5-9	Criminality and Class/Status Linkages	97
5-10	Three-Variable Path Model	98
5-11	Time Sequences in the General Race-Disposition Model	99

List of Tables

3-1	Type of College Attended by Judicial Race	49
3-2	Type of Law School Attended by Judicial Race	50
3-3	Black Metro City Judges—Years Admitted to Law School and Type of Law School Attended	51
3-4	Prejudicial Career Positions by Judicial Race	52
4-1	Determinations of Guilt by Race of Judge and Race of Defendant	66
4-2	Determinations of Guilt by Individual Judge	67
4-3	Determinations of Guilt by Individual Judge and by Race of Defendant	68
4-4	Mean Sentence Severity by Race of Judge and Race of Defendant	70
4-5	Individual Judicial Differences in Sentence Severity—Percentage Deviations from Mean Sentence	71
4-6	Mean Sentence Severity by Individual Judge and by Race of Defendant	72
5-1	Percentage of Defendants Convicted by Race in Selected Crime Categories	79
5-2	Percentage of Defendants Jailed by Race in Selected Crime Categories	80
5-3	Mean Sentence Severity by Race in Selected Crime Categories	81
5-4	Independent Variables Included in the Path Analysis	88
5-5	Variables Included in the Race-Sentencing Path Model	90
5-6	Reduced Race-Sentencing Model—Significant Pathways of Influence	93

Preface

On more than one occasion I have been asked what qualifies me, a white, first-generation American, the son of German immigrants, to write about the black American's struggle before the law. For those more concerned about who I am than what I say, no reply will suffice. For others who are more curious, I can truthfully answer that as a child I was taught the evils of discrimination by my parents. I grew up to reject the concept as much as those who discriminate reject the people they hate and fear. However, my feelings about bias were not qualified by race, religion, or nationality. So my initial scholarly interest about the human condition of man hating his fellow man for essentially irrational reasons was, in fact, color-blind. When applied to the most serious social and political problems in the United States, these more general interests quickly focused on race. As a political scientist studying the legal process, an almost natural outgrowth of these concerns was this book on the backgrounds and sentencing behavior of black judges and the treatment of black defendants in a trial court.

Several years ago a fellow political scientist cautioned me to stay away from this research. He suggested, in effect, that I study white judges and leave these topics to a black political scientist. To me, a racial criterion of any sort is no more acceptable as a prerequisite for this project than it is as a guide to judicial selection or defendant sentencing. I hope that this personal conviction is supported by a fair-minded analysis of the difficult and sensitive questions examined here.

Acknowledgments

I am extremely grateful to friends and colleagues who have provided invaluable assistance and advice during the course of this study. Joel Glassman, Bob Holsworth, Carol Kohfeld, Russell Smith, Charlie Williams, Donna Corno, and Beth Uhlman made helpful suggestions that improved the entire manuscript. In my moments of doubt, Richard J. Richardson encouraged me to see the project through to completion. Judges and court personnel in Metro City freely gave of their time to answer my many questions. The University of Missouri-St. Louis generously funded various portions of the project. Because their interest in seeing this book completed was nearly as great as mine, the office crew led by Debbie Dodson made me continue writing to meet deadlines. Their typing, editorial assistance, and genuine concern for the book will always be appreciated. Finally, I am grateful to the Western Political Science Association, the University of Texas Press, and Holt, Rinehart and Winston for permission to incorporate portions of my work which they published in preliminary form.[1] Regrettably, any errors not caught by my friends remain my responsibility.

Note

1. "Race, Recruitment and Representation: Background Differences between Black and White Trial Court Judges," *Western Political Quarterly* 30 (December 1977):457-470; "Black Elite Decision Making: The Case of Trial Judges," *American Journal of Political Science* 22, no. 4 (November 1978):884-895 © 1978 by the University of Texas Press; "The Impact of Defendant Race in Trial Court Sanctioning Decisions," in *Public Law and Public Policy,* ed. John A. Gardiner, pp. 19-51 (New York: Praeger, 1977). Copyright © 1977 by Praeger Publishers, Inc. Reprinted by permission of Holt, Rinehart and Winston.

Racial Justice

1 Race and the Legal Process

Racial differences among people in the United States have posed the most serious domestic problems we have faced as a nation. Political and military battles have been fought over the degree to which members of racial and ethnic groups would be free to determine their own destiny and the destiny of the country by participating in the governing process. At times, bias in legislative and executive decision making at the local, state, and national levels has benefited some while systematically discriminating against the less fortunate and powerful. Historically, black Americans have been among the least privileged.

Blacks have not suffered solely at the hands of biased executives and legislators. The legal process in general and courts of law in particular share responsibility for creating and perpetuating racial inequities. Slavery was legitimized and Jim Crow laws were upheld in courts. A "separate but equal" social order began as a legal fiction. Courts oppressed blacks through the creative application of the law. In more recent times, the judicial system has worked toward an opposite end. Examples of racial progress receiving their initial and often only governmental support in the courts include school desegregation, expanded employment and educational opportunities, and lessened bias in important policy areas such as public accommodations and transportation. Overall, a balanced evaluation would probably yield both harsh criticism and some praise in assessing the involvement of courts in what Myrdal called America's great dilemma.[1]

This book is an inquiry into the relationship between courts and race. Several distinct racial issues are examined within the bounds of a single court. Before turning to these topics, we can categorize race questions in the legal process broadly along two distinguishable, though interrelated, dimensions. The internal dimension encompasses the causes and consequences of black underrepresentation in various positions within the legal elite, whereas the external dimension emphasizes the more frequently discussed subject of discriminatory decisions of courts. To the extent that they are supported, charges of exclusionary practices and racially biased decision making represent a basic denial to black Americans of fair treatment either on or before the bench of justice.

Both of these race problems are studied in the context of a major urban trial court. The black judiciary provides the internal focus, and black defendants an external focus. Specifically, interest centers on the backgrounds and behavior of sixteen black judges and the treatment accorded over 34,000 black felony defendants. By examining case decisions and making comparisons to appropriate white judge and defendant groups, we can determine whether "race makes a difference" in this court and, if so, exactly what the differences are.[2]

Before we detail specific avenues of inquiry, it is worthwhile to assess both topics more comprehensively. Such an overview is free from the narrowness that inevitably results from working with a single court or data set. Moreover, a general discussion of both the judge and defendant race questions provides a framework around which the subsequent analysis can be structured. Because the black judiciary is drawn from the black legal community and the professional problems of both groups have been so closely intertwined, their efforts to achieve equal opportunities in the law must be examined together. We begin by describing an issue that by itself merits investigation—the continuing problem of black legal underrepresentation.

Black Legal and Judicial Underrepresentation

Evidence

Black Americans have been and remain underrepresented in decision-making positions throughout the legal system. Blacks are notably absent in police forces, correctional staffs, and middle- and top-level administrative posts.[3] Nowhere, however, is this underrepresentation more pronounced than in membership in the legal profession itself. The dearth of black legal talent is evident at the key entry point to the profession—law school—and subsequently in the practicing bar and judiciary.

Recent progress does not alter the fundamental conclusion that law school opportunities have been sharply restricted for blacks. Only a handful of blacks graduated from predominantly white law schools before 1950. Prior to that time, black law schools represented the only alternative. Nineteen were established in the 1800s, but eighteen failed to survive the century. The one that did, Howard University School of Law, represented the preeminent source for black legal training until the late 1930s and 1940s; other black law schools were hastily established at that time in hopes of evading integration in white, state law schools anticipated as the result of Supreme Court rulings.[4] Prior to the sudden emergence of these black, state law schools, approximately twenty black law students constituted the national graduating "class" each year. Between 1940 and 1950, fifty to one hundred students at most graduated every year.

In the 1950s an era of tokenism in white law schools began that continued into the late 1960s, according to some, and to the present day according to others. The few blacks accepted in predominantly white law schools and those who entered black law schools vastly underrepresented the black population. As recently as 1965, officials at Harvard Law School estimated that there were no more than 700 blacks among the 65,000 students studying law in the United

States.[5] These figures translate into a black law student enrollment of just over 1 percent, compared to a black population of 12 percent nationally.

Greater sensitivity to discriminatory practices coupled with affirmative action programs has increased black opportunities in white law schools significantly in recent years. But even today, enrollment figures signal progress only when contrasted to a dismal past. By 1970 the number of black law students had risen to 2,100, and by 1974 it had more than doubled again to 4,800. Yet during this time, overall law school enrollments were increasing nearly as rapidly to total over 100,00 by 1974. So even this expanded pool of black law students (still less than 5 percent of the total) significantly underrepresents the black population proportionally.

Limited black legal training has meant a scarcity of practicing black attorneys.[6] Prior to 1900, some 200 to 300 were active at any time. By 1910 this figure had risen to 800, but thirty years later the national total had increased to only 1,000. Recent data do not paint a much brighter picture. In 1950, 1,450 black attorneys were practicing law; in 1960, 2,200; and in 1970, 4,200. Black membership in bar associations, ranging between 0.6 and 1.5 percent of the total, consistently has been less than the already minimal enrollments of blacks in law school.

In 1970 there were about 325,000 attorneys practicing law in the United States. Legal services for the black and white communities, however, were hardly equally available, with 1 white in 625 an attorney compared to 1 black in 7,000.[7] If one accepts the principle of proportional representation, an immediate increase of *30,000* black attorneys is required to equalize the legal talent available to both subpopulations.

A paucity of black jurists is no surprise given the degree of black underrepresentation apparent in both law school and legal practice. Black exclusion from the judiciary was almost total until 1950; fewer than two dozen had served in any judicial capacity during the preceding century.[8] In the twenty-five years that followed, and particularly during the past decade, advances have been recorded. But again this progress is relative, and recent evidence indicates that existing inequities remain large. Various estimates of the current black judicial population have been made.[9] While no two agree, the consensus is that there are still fewer than 350 black judges presiding in either federal or state courts throughout the country. Even by using the higher estimates, blacks still comprise under 1.5 percent of the nation's judicial strength.

Equally important in evaluating the black bench is the significance of the judicial posts blacks have attained. Of their already small numbers, approximately seventy-five, or at least 20 percent, hold minor positions such as justice of the peace or traffic court judge.[10] Although the number of black federal and state trial and appellate judges has increased slowly, these inferior black judicial posts tend to diminish still further the influence of the black bench.

A third characteristic of the black judiciary is the location of most judgeships. The South affords blacks few opportunities; until 1978 there were no black federal judges and only a dozen or so black state-court jurists. Since a majority of black Americans still live in the South, the degree of black judicial underrepresentation there is staggering. Outside the South black jurists are found primarily in major metropolitan areas. In fact, more than 50 percent of them preside in New York City, Chicago, Detroit, Los Angeles, Philadelphia, and Washington. Not even in these large cities, however, are blacks proportionately represented. Beverly Blair Cook describes black judicial underrepresentation in Northern states and cities which can be made to look "good" only when compared to the virtual absence of a Southern black bench.[11]

After being limited numerically and by type of position, black judges are also found restricted by geographic region. Overall, the judiciary is one of the decision-making positions that black Americans find most difficult to attain. Therefore, an important and obvious component of the race issue within the legal order is the limited black opportunities to practice and preside in our courts of law.

Causes

This exclusionary pattern has been so effective that one must wonder whether a coordinated strategy was in effect. Although the evidence does not reveal such a scheme, a series of barriers and hurdles woven loosely together in the fabric of our national history has acted as an effective screening mechanism. In the past these obstacles eliminated, and today they still greatly diminish, the opportunity for black Americans to complete law school, become successful practitioners, and finally attain judicial positions.

Inferior black academic preparation in elementary and secondary schools has severely restricted subsequent legal opportunities. Wide racial disparities in both achievement and ability are frequently evident well before students entertain thoughts of a higher education.[12] Early handicaps hamper and often deter later efforts. Effects are cumulative and results predictable: a limited pool of black applicants to colleges and law schools and subsequent difficulties in succeeding once admitted. A survey of law school deans conducted by the Association of American Law Schools reported poor academic preparation as one of the main reasons blacks failed admittance,[13] while one dean emphasized weak educational backgrounds generally and a poor command of English specifically as the principal stumbling blocks to black success.[14] Law school "headstart" programs such as the one established by the Council on Legal Education Opportunity (CLEO) and race-sensitive admissions policies have not eliminated basic educational deficiencies as a barrier to the legal profession for blacks.

Doubtless, difficulties prior to law school are attractive explanations for some as the primary causes of black underrepresentation in the legal profession. But historical evidence and the ever-increasing number of educationally well-prepared black students indicate other factors at work. Two have been entrance requirements of questionable validity coupled with past admissions practices designed to preclude black attendance.

Considerable controversy surrounds the criteria established by law schools to determine the quality of student applicants. In addition to a continuing debate over the correlation between the standard entrance device, the Law School Admission Test (LSAT), and law school achievement, concern is expressed over the potential handicap this test poses for minority group students. It is argued that the qualifications necessary to become a successful community lawyer differ substantially from those required of attorneys pursuing more traditional, corporate legal work. Entrance examinations structured along this corporate dimension, as the LSAT is alleged to be, will fail to measure the potential for success in the type of community legal practice that many minority group law students wish to pursue. Perhaps even more serious is a second contention that the black and white subcultures in this country differ significantly enough that the LSAT, a potentially accurate predictor of white success in law school, is unable to gauge black competence.[15]

Ernest Gellhorn views the current legal environment as being shaped by a "legacy of past discriminatory practices."[16] Nowhere is such a judgment more appropriate than in the exclusionary admissions policies adopted by predominantly white law schools years ago that continued, though modified to suit the times, well into the 1960s.[17] Until 1964, some law schools still voluntarily reported denying admission to applicants based on a racial criterion. Gentleman's agreements were more common and more insidious but just as effective in excluding blacks completely or admitting them in token numbers.

By the end of the 1960s efforts to equalize minority group opportunities had begun.[18] Recruitment drives to solicit black applications were undertaken, and the CLEO program was launched. Although these efforts represent movement in an antidiscriminatory direction, disparities and inequities are still great. For example, the oftenpraised CLEO project with a $700,000 budget and the active participation of several of the country's major law schools and foundations had a very modest goal of adding 300 minority group lawyers to the profession by 1973. The inadequacy of this program is readily apparent given the need for 30,000 new black attorneys to achieve proportional representation. While certainly a positive step, the program becomes hardly noticeable given the magnitude of the problem.

If the difficulties faced in qualifying for and gaining admittance to law school do not pose insurmountable obstacles, more immediate causes of black underrepresentation are found in the experiences of many blacks in law school and subsequent legal practice. Inadequate financial support is a burden that has been borne by all but the most recent black law graduates. Traditionally, few scholarships have been available to students training for what is thought to be a financially rewarding profession. Ignored were those from economically disadvantaged backgrounds who had neither family wealth at their command nor the creditworthiness necessary to secure a loan. The Shuman survey of black lawyers reveals that nearly 75 percent of the attorneys queried needed to work while in law school, a circumstance that hindered their scholastic efforts and adversely affected their general educational experiences.[19] Moreover, economic considerations may have eliminated the legal profession entirely for some. High black law school attrition rates have been partly attributed to financial problems,[20] while Shuman observes that professional careers requiring only an undergraduate degree are becoming increasingly attractive to qualified blacks.[21]

Other handicaps facing black law students pertain to the type and quality of the education they receive. Black law schools may be better able to respond to the needs of black students, as some claim,[22] but many of these schools are hard-pressed financially and do not carry strong reputations within the legal profession. With one or two exceptions, they are unable to provide top-quality libraries, teaching faculties, and placement programs. In fact, Atlanta's black mayor, Maynard Jackson, has stated flatly that black law schools are inferior to predominantly white institutions.[23] Unfortunately, it is often questionable how much better off black students are if they can and do choose to attend a white law school.

Considerable criticism has been directed toward the curricula in many predominantly white institutions. The charge is that courses are irrelevant to many black lawyers' community orientations, in addition to frequently ignoring the social context in which the law functions.[24] The dearth of black law professors poses another problem. In 1968 fewer than half a dozen were teaching in white law schools across the country. Their absence was painfully evident because black students feel that professors often do not understand their needs. The inability or unwillingness of white teachers to make a sincere effort to see the world and legal issues from the black viewpoint is considered a primary cause of these students' failure to "adjust" to law school.[25]

Adjustment problems have plagued black law students in other ways. Until relatively recently, three or four admissions represented the limited commitment white schools had to providing blacks a legal education. This tokenism presented formidable problems for blacks trying to learn in this environment. Included were the difficult and potentially unhealthy burdens of either ignoring race issues completely or resolving them by trying to gain acceptance as virtual carbon copies of their white peers.[26] Frequently acceptance did not come, and many blacks turned to the dysfunctional and in some ways self-destructive task of trying to prove their abilities to white classmates and instructors.[27] The intense pressures to respond to the law school challenge in this manner persisted as long as black students were only able to achieve a quality legal education in what for them was an artificial environment—nearly all white.

Blacks have often confronted other barriers upon graduation regardless of the type of law school attended. The first is passing a state bar examination. Black failure rates continue to exceed those of whites by a sizable margin with discrimination and inadequate preparation offered as explanations.[28] Other problems have become less serious over time. Professional opportunities were sharply restricted as blacks were officially or unofficially barred from various legal associations and organizations, including the American Bar Association. This exclusion damaged prospects for a successful career as important social and professional contacts, referral services, specialized libraries, and research aids were systematically denied to black attorneys. These disadvantages were often compounded by the young black attorney's inability to be considered for desirable clerkships and, more importantly, employment by predominantly white firms.[29] Today opportunities in the white legal, business, and government worlds exist for the *top* black law graduates. Whether these commitments will extend over time, develop into more than token hiring, and include a cross section of all black graduates is far from certain at present.

Denied access to the white legal establishment, black attorneys tried to succeed exclusively within the black community. Their attempts often failed because of economic difficulties. The capital needed to start a law firm was not available to newly trained black lawyers. Forced to struggle on their own or participate in temporary office-sharing arrangements, they frequently faced the virtually impossible task of working other jobs while trying to build a practice; this challenge proved too great for many. Somewhat surprisingly, progressive social reforms have also had unintended negative consequences on black attorneys active in criminal, negligence, and domestic relations matters. No-fault automobile insurance, no-fault divorce laws, and the expansion of public defenders' offices have all lessened the need for legal services within the black community.[30]

The most serious economic problems, however, derive from characteristics of the black population itself. Poverty, marginal jobs, and minimum wages mean many black clients will not be able to pay a lawyer's fee. Just as importantly, blacks often lack faith in black attorneys; so when they need legal help, they turn to white lawyers. This decision frequently stems from a realistic appraisal of the career disadvantages that black attorneys face; there is apprehension that the black lawyer will have inferior legal training, have less than adequate library and research facilities at his disposal, and, most significantly, have less "clout" in the courtroom than white attorneys.[31] The problem is painfully described by a prominent black community leader: "The black American ... conceives of the black attorney as the Calhoun of 'Amos and Andy.' To the black lawyer he has taken the crumbs of litigation, while to our white counterpart he has tendered the full loaf."[32]

Judicial recruitment opportunities are not shared equally among groups in society. No better example of this inequity is found than in black judicial selection. Not only must the future black jurist clear all the hurdles black lawyers face, but he must then also contend with additional obstacles unique to his prospective post. The most serious is minimal black participation in the politics of judicial selection. Shortcomings within the black community are apparently responsible in part. "The importance of the judiciary generally," contends Judge George Crockett of the Recorders' Court in Detroit, "and the awesomeness of the power that judges wield in American life is a fact that seems to have been readily grasped by every minority group except non-whites."[33] More compelling evidence, however, points to exclusionary barriers thrown up by the white legal establishment.

By restricting black involvement in bar association matters, black attorneys had been effectively removed from deliberations regarding endorsements to the bench. Since the bar frequently selects the type of person to serve, if not the specific individual, minimal black input here reduces or eliminates pressure to make the judiciary racially representative. More damaging, though harder to document, is strong resistance to a black judiciary by white officials. Judicial decisions influence political, social, and economic relationships in society. Considering the sensitivity of a judicial post, resistance by some whites to increased black judicial power is not surprising. Judge Crockett sees this opposition as being inspired by fear:

> Many of us are convinced that this relative paucity of black judges and the frantic effort to block the election or appointment of more, stems from the fear in some quarters that this awesome state power which inheres in the trial judge will be used by black judges to correct many of the racist and classist practices of our judicial system.[34]

While this resistance has become less intense recently, black underrepresentation on the bench and in the bar is not a random occurrence. Convincing evidence leads to the conclusion that it is the result of a systematic denial of opportunity. Rooted in history and continuing, though partially abated, to the present, numerous obstacles encompassing the entirety of a legal career have served as an effective screening mechanism to circumscribe black participation in the legal system.

Consequences

Despite these inequities, black legal underrepresentation could merely pose a disturbing moral dilemma in that the absence of black lawyers and judges has not yet been shown to distort the legal system, or their presence to improve it. The consequences of this underrepresentation become much more serious when we examine the contributions made by the relatively small number of black lawyers and judges active today. In pressing for social change through the law, black attorneys may be more effective than their white counterparts in championing unpopular causes or defending controversial clients. This is particularly true when black interests are involved, as they often are. The civil rights struggle represents a continuing example in this regard; the black lawyer frequently possesses the unique advantages of being able to understand the background and facts of a case through personal experience, feel deeply committed to a broader purpose, and work effectively within the black community.[35]

Courts of law, however, do not function primarily to bring about major social change. In large measure the quality of justice is shaped by thousands of unpublicized, relatively routine civil and criminal decisions affecting individual litigants on a case-by-case basis. In what may be perceived as a more mundane arena, the special attributes of the black advocate also are essential. Myrdal was one of the first to realize the importance of black legal counsel to a black client.[36] His conclusions have been echoed frequently but by no one more forcefully than James Montgomery, a prominent black attorney. "The black man may see as his advocate a white person who means well but there is not a white man living who can understand a black client as a black man can. There is no way to infuse the soul of oppression into a man."[37] With their empathy, knowledge, and commitment, black attorneys play important roles in shaping the justness of the legal product—be it a major social initiative or a minor criminal offense.

The black attorney can also become a significant figure within the black community generally. For too long black powerlessness has confirmed pervasive feelings of black inferiority. The cumulative effect of frequent interactions between black citizens and dominant white elites has been a series of derogatory stereotypes held by blacks of themselves. By their presence alone black attorneys challenge such negative self-images; they are visible proof of black success in penetrating a previously restricted professional circle. An active and visible black legal fraternity can serve as a much needed source of community pride and inspiration.[38]

Black judges also play significant roles in and out of the courtroom. By being at the pinnacle of the legal profession, they are able to make several contributions unique to their positions. Because of their uncommon judicial backgrounds and experiences, blacks provide diversity on the bench that often encompasses different and, some argue, challenging perspectives on the law and legal system.[39] Part of this differing perspective appears to be a deeply held commitment to constructive change. Judge Joseph Howard expresses this view rather eloquently and in so doing echoes the thoughts of several black colleagues:

As blacks we know the poignancy of the law and as judges we know its power. As black judges, then, we bear a heavy responsibility for improving the quality of justice for all people, especially, but not exclusively our own.... The modified judicial ethic that has been forged in the crucible of the black experience has given us a unique capacity to restate the law, redefine justice, and present views from a different perspective.[40]

One specific change taking place is an attack on discriminatory practices in the court. "We have got to be there," states Judge A. Leon Higgenbotham, "we have got to be a counterbalancing influence, to point out to others what have been highly significant, unarticulated premises which are often absolutely racist."[41] These premises can influence nearly every decision made from arrest to imprisonment. For example, they may exist as stereotypical attitudes held by police and other court personnel about the propensity of blacks to commit crime. They may take shape as subtle redefinitions of due process in an era of court delay. Or they may be evident as ignorance of the economic bias inherent in the bail/bond system. Knowing proper legal procedure and the full array of defendant rights and having authority within their courts, black judges can challenge, if not change, discriminatory presumptions such as these as they impinge on court activity.

Black judges, like black attorneys, claim a particular sensitivity to the problems faced by minority defendants in and out of the courtroom.[42] Often derived from similar childhood and other life experiences, this sensitivity coupled with an awareness of biases in the legal process yields a distinctive configuration of attributes and attitudes that may make blacks uniquely qualified as court reformers. Many black judges are cognizant of their special role in this regard. Witness Judge Crockett: "I think a black judge ... has got to be a reformist—he cannot be a member of the club. The whole purpose of selecting him is that the people are dissatisfied with the status quo and they want him to shake it up, and his role is to shake it up."[43] Elsewhere he continues: "I will not be part of the in-bred and self-perpetuating 'arrangement' for handling black and poor arrestees ... which permeate[s] the very air surrounding our criminal trial courts."[44]

One direct way of reducing judicial racism is by increasing white judges' perception of blatant as well as subtle discriminatory practices. Sensitizing their white colleagues along these lines is seen by many black judges as an integral part of their reform mission. Indicative is Judge Crockett's experience during the 1968 Detroit riot. While white judges were setting uniformly high bail ($10,000) for suspected rioters, Crockett established a "low bail" policy. After two days, the other justices followed his example by reducing bail levels substantially, indicating to him that "... one black judge who shows the disparity between treatment of whites and blacks can set the pattern for his white brothers."[45] In addition to setting behavioral examples, black judges can effectively "educate" their white colleagues through formal and informal meetings and discussions. The Judicial Council of the National Bar Association organized with this as a primary objective, and black jurists also report progress in talking with other judges on an individual basis.[46] Thus, by both their actions and personal influence, black judges may become the racial consciences of their courts and have a significant, positive impact on the overall administration of justice.

The importance of a black judiciary is not strictly confined to the courtroom. The black legal fraternity may reap substantial benefits from the presence of black judges. We have commented on the serious economic difficulties facing black attorneys because they are considered ineffective by many potential black clients. The sitting black judge may be able to change this assessment according to knowledgeable black judges and lawyers. Judge Robert Evans comments almost matter-of-factly, "Now that there are some black judges, especially in the cities, black attorneys will get clients."[47] Admittedly increased patronage, should it occur, will result more from a feeling in the black community that black attorneys will have more clout than from actual preferential treatment. But even if the belief is only that their race will no longer be held against them, black attorneys are bound to benefit. So the long-term economic viability of the community legal practice for black attorneys may depend, in part at least, on black success in attaining judicial positions.

The black judicial presence also has wider consequences within the black community. Until recently, the nonwhite litigant would encounter white faces virtually without exception during every stage of legal proceedings. Based on this experience, it comes as no surprise that some blacks have questioned the impartiality and even the legitimacy of a legal order that has excluded them.[48] For those who have nearly lost faith in the American ideal, the black judge is a symbol of hope and encouragement. The significance of this special judicial role is powerfully stated by one black jurist:

> He [the black judge] is a symbol of all we hold dear in this country—he is a symbol of American democracy... and that... is perhaps the highest role the black judge plays—in being a symbol of law and order with justice insofar as the poor and underprivileged in our society are concerned.[49]

Finally, the black judge may have a significant psychological impact in the white community as well. Differential occupational status has been an important factor in creating and maintaining racial prejudice largely because the jobs most blacks hold are at or near the bottom of the job ladder.[50] One beneficial effect of any increase in black occupational prestige may, therefore, be a reduction in prejudicial attitudes of whites which is a factor contributing to inferior employment opportunities for blacks in the first place.[51] As a result of the visibility and stature of a judicial position, the influence of the black judiciary in countering these harmful stereotypes could be marked.

Clearly, the issues that surround black representation within the legal profession in general and the judiciary in particular raise more than abstract, moral questions. The underrepresentation that is found has serious implications for the individual defendant, the legal system, and society as a whole because meaningful black participation is seen as improving the quality and enhancing the effective function of the legal process. In the end, the solution to underrepresentation is as obvious as the problem itself: expand black opportunities within the legal and judicial professions. Recently some successes along these lines have been achieved. This book assesses the consequences of this success by investigating the black judge—the newest influential black political elite.

Race from the Defendant's Perspective

Race is a consideration in the legal process along a second, equally serious, dimension. Charges are common that discrimination, directly attributable to the decisions of judges and other legal personnel, denies black citizens the full and equal protection of the law. Although evidence based on recent research is neither entirely consistent nor totally conclusive, historically discrimination was both extreme and widespread.

The human tragedy that was slavery has been well documented. What has not been as frequently recorded was the necessary involvement of the courts and the law in the establishment and perpetuation of the institution.[52] Colonial legislatures legally distinguished black slaves from white indentured servants, making bondage for blacks a lifetime, hereditary condition. The Founding Fathers made racism a cornerstone of our legal structure via Constitutional provisions counting blacks as three-fifths of a person, sanctioning the slave trade, and requiring the return of runaway slaves.[53] In the South, slave codes denied virtually all human dignity to blacks and rendered them legal nonpersons, prohibiting them from bringing suit and testifying while subjecting them to a much harsher brand of criminal justice. In the North, the law freed blacks but kept them inferior by denying them employment, education, and the right to vote. The Dred Scott decision describes the essence of blacks' relationship to the law prior to the Civil War; legally they were chattel.[54] As one historian concluded, "... the judicial process was utilized in every instance, not to let justice be done but to minimize liberty and to increase and sanction the brutality, the utter brutality, of slavery."[55]

The abolition of slavery ended neither discriminatory behavior nor the legal establishment's involvement in it. Instead, slavery left a racist legacy which ultimately triumphed over reform efforts. The Fourteenth and Fifteenth Amendments along with the Civil Rights Acts of 1866 and 1875, the Enforcement Act of 1870, and the Anti-Ku Klux Klan Act of 1871 were seriously undermined by post-Civil War Supreme Court rulings such as *Bylew* v. *U.S.* and

The Civil Rights Cases.[56] Jim Crow laws effectively maintained a segregated Southern society which was further legitimized by the Court in *Plessy* v. *Ferguson.*[57]

In many ways then, the South won in the courts what it lost on the battlefield. Typical was the treatment of black defendants. "... when the black man happens to be on trial," wrote Frederick Douglass in 1883, "... he will find all presumptions of law against him. It is not so much the business of his enemies to prove him guilty, as it is the job of himself to prove his innocence."[58] The harsh post-Civil War reality for blacks was a legal structure selectively and negatively applied to them. Little changed during the next half century. Through violence, underprotection, and the disregard of their formal, legal rights, blacks were given ample reason to feel that there were indeed justice and law—justice and law applicable only to whites.

Based on this rather sordid history, recent reports alleging that racial distinctions still exist throughout the legal process are not surprising. Although these charges do not go unchallenged,[59] bias is said to permeate nearly all administrative, civil, and criminal proceedings.[60] Research on the enforcement of criminal laws has shown differential treatment from arrest to imprisonment. Blacks are subjected to greater scrutiny by police, contributing in turn to higher arrest rates. Arrest is followed by an increased likelihood of prosecution and more limited opportunities to post bail and to plea bargain. At trial, blacks are claimed to be found guilty more often than white defendants similarly situated. Once in prison, blacks are judged by different, more exacting standards and find parole more difficult to achieve than whites.[61] The harshest critics proclaim that in practice very little has changed for the black citizen-defendant-prisoner since slavery.[62]

One ready explanation for these race-related inequities is the racist attitudes of legal decisionmakers. Typical is the conclusion that public officials, under the influence of their prejudices, tend to make decisions that exaggerate black criminality.[63] Other interpretations are not as straightforward and bring into play race-related economic, social, and political distinctions evident in society generally.

Demographic data reveal that as a group blacks are more likely to be poor and less likely to be well educated than whites. Poverty, in turn, is associated with crime, especially property offenses and particularly the types of crime that lead to arrest and harsh sanctions. The common thief stands a much better chance of being caught and punished than does the sophisticated, white-collar criminal; and more often than not in this country, the thief is black. This relationship has been used to downplay race as a factor contributing to dispositional inequities. Not so says Derrick Bell: "Since race and socioeconomic status interact in such a complex of ways, the claim that poverty but not race is the operative factor is, in effect, not to say much of any significance when it is recognized that those who are poor are so often non-white."[64]

Socioeconomic disadvantages hurt blacks in other ways. Most middle- and upper-class people charged with crimes are as unaware of the law as are lower-class persons, but they can pay for quality legal counsel to represent them.[65] Poor blacks cannot. This financial handicap coupled with a lack of knowledge about the need for competent counsel frequently places blacks in unfavorable positions to assert their rights or strike advantageous bargains with court personnel.[66]

We have seen how in the past the law became a powerful political weapon used to oppress blacks. Today the law continues to have political utility as a means of maintaining the position and advantage of the current political, economic, and social elite. For example, preferential treatment for business interests might be evident as initial police or subsequent judicial disregard of local ordinances thought to retard trade (for example, double-parking restrictions). Selective enforcement of vagrancy and disorderly conduct statutes to rid the community of so-called undesirables is another example. When laws and the legal mechanism are used for such purposes, blacks usually fare poorly. Their demands for reform or perhaps even their very presence in a community challenges the status quo, and as a group they usually lack the requisite political power to control or redefine the mission of law enforcement agencies to their advantage.[67]

Power and privilege may also influence the daily decisions made by court personnel in another way. Facilities and staff are heavily overburdened in many jurisdictions with no budgetary relief or docket reductions in sight. Rapid case disposition becomes an organizational necessity in this environment. Also perceived as necessary is some selectivity in the type of individual subject to the firm hand of the law. Lacking procedural knowledge, fearful and often unable to afford counsel, the poor and otherwise disadvantaged offer little resistance to the complex, confusing, and harsh reality of legal proceedings. The bias is obvious: an effective policy intended to maximize political benefits yet minimize organizational strains emphasizes vigorous law enforcement efforts against blacks who are frequently both politically weak and less likely to be cognizant of the full scope of their due-process rights.[68]

Finally, a cultural gap frequently exists between the poor, black defendant and middle-class court officials. False stereotyping of minorities is one damaging consequence of this cultural distance. Another is simply the inability of the legal elite to identify with the disadvantaged defendant. The President's Crime Commission observed:

> Most city prosecutors and judges... can easily mistake a certain manner of dress or speech, alien or repugnant to them but ordinary enough in the defendant's world, as an index of moral worthlessness. They can mistake ignorance or fear of the law as indifference to it.[69]

Subsequent actions can be negatively affected by legal decisionmakers' inaccurate perceptions of black litigants or their circumstances. As noted earlier, narrowing this cultural gulf represents one of the most persuasive arguments for increasing black participation within the legal elite.[70]

Having now come full circle, we can better appreciate the difficulty in distinguishing the components of the general race issue in the legal process for other than analytical purposes. At many points specific racial issues intersect, and this overlap itself attests to the seriousness of a problem that encompasses actions within decision-making agencies, actions emanating from these agencies, and their wider societal impacts. The significance of the topic is attributable not only to its scope but also to the basic questions of justice and equality that are at stake. To the extent that limitations on participation in the legal profession exist, blacks are denied the right to contribute to the application and interpretation of laws affecting them. The race issue also includes discriminatory decisions, victimizing one group of citizens by the imposition of unwarranted legal sanctions. The presence of bias and prejudice in the very agencies of government intended to check them can be seen both as a fundamental weakness in our polity and as a challenge to understand, confront, and in the end reform the legal process.

A Study of Race in the U.S. Legal Process

If the race issues discussed here present a challange for society, they are equally challenging to scholars. The challenge becomes even more compelling given calls for additional research. Emanating from both the black community and a relatively small band of investigators, these requests stress the urgent need for thorough, scientific, and methodologically sophisticated work in the area.[71] Responding in part at least to such requests, this book proceeds down a few of the many paths of inquiry deserving exploration. Drawing on an unusually rich collection of data from the trial court in a community referred to as Metro City, we undertake a comparative study of black judges and black defendants in the context of the felony disposition process.

Aware of the treacherous path black Americans must travel in gaining admittance to the legal profession and the judiciary, it is of considerable importance in both theoretical and practical terms to learn as much as possible about the origins and careers of those few who have succeeded. Chapter 3 represents such an inquiry for the sixteen black trial court judges in Metro City. The availability of detailed autobiographical statements completed by these judges along with those of seventy-nine of their white colleagues enables us to pose two fundamental questions regarding this unique political elite: What are the precursors of black judicial success and how representative is the black bench? Answers are derived by describing the black judiciary and also comparing it to the white bench by judicial birthplace, educational achievements, prejudicial careers, political activity, and methods of selection.

A judgeship is a personal triumph for any attorney; it is the crowning achievement of a legal career. In light of the handicaps that blacks have had to overcome, black judicial success becomes even more remarkable. Because of their small numbers and recent arrival on the bench, judicial scholars know little about these remarkable men and women. Most information about their experience is drawn from the writings of individual black judges. While extremely insightful, this material lacks generality. By systematically exploring the backgrounds and careers of a large contingent of black jurists, we can begin to define the meaning of "blackness" on the bench.

Does the racial factor encompass an entire set of distinguishable background and career characteristics? How do the similarities or differences that emerge affect the representation which the black community receives? In other words, does racial diversity on this court signal diversity in other aspects of the judicial personality and experience? This expectation provides much of the force behind repeated calls for more equitable group representation within various policy-making elites. The issues of descriptive and substantive representation are closely tied to the question of leadership recruitment. Are there official and, just as importantly, unofficial prerequisites for judicial office in Metro City that differ by race? If so, how do the standards compare and do they, in general, act to restrict sharply the diversity and hence the representativeness of the black bench?

These broader issues can be approached through a set of specific interracial comparisons. By placing a person in a position to establish contacts and visibility, local origins and continuing community ties become important factors in judicial recruitment in many jurisdictions. If found in Metro City, a localism prerequisite may further reduce the already small pool of eligible black judicial candidates, given the relatively recent, large-scale movement of blacks out of the South. The quality of the educations received by future black and white judges is also contrasted. Do educational standards differ by race, and, if so, what are their parameters? Since blacks are underrepresented numerically, we may hypothesize that judgeships, to the extent that they are available, can be restricted to blacks holding only the most impeccable credentials—credentials perhaps significantly better than those of their future white colleagues. An educational prerequisite could also be graduation from a predominantly white college and/or law school. This informal requirement would further limit judicial opportunities to a small subset of the already restricted black legal elite.

Difficulties in establishing and maintaining a viable legal practice for blacks may be reflected in different prejudicial careers and activities. Extensive political involvement and government employment, particularly in a prosecutorial capacity, may be more in evidence for blacks compared to corporate work and law firm affiliations for whites. Types of professional and community service activities would also be expected to differ. Blacks' civil rights activities are of particular interest since extensive involvement might make prospective candidates less attractive to members of the legal and political establishments instrumental in recruitment. This issue is but one of several that surround the process of judicial selection. A lively debate continues over whether blacks benefit more from elective or appointive selection systems.[72] Judicial recruitment in Metro City and state has both elective and appointive features, thus providing a good setting to examine these alternatives.

The significance of this background investigation derives largely from the importance of judicial decision making. Judges' rulings, arrived at either independently or in conjunction with other court actors, often determine guilt or innocence and almost invariably establish punishment guidelines in trial courts. There are a variety of persuasive arguments for expanding the black judiciary. Few, however, incorporate a discussion of how black judges may differ from whites in carrying out their critical job of actually deciding cases. Chapter 4 examines this rather delicate political/legal question by systematically contrasting the verdicts and sentences handed down by black and white judges in over 30,000 felony cases.

Limited debate on black judicial decision making is not surprising. Members of dominant institutions have resisted sharing meaningful authority with blacks not only because it would lessen their own power but also out of fear that blacks would not exercise power wisely or well.[73] In the judicial context this means apprehension that black judges would be incompetent, play racial favorites, or both. Today these fears cannot be proclaimed openly. Unfortunately, those advocating broader black representation cannot respond to these unspoken charges directly because no reliable data on the subject exist. One article predicts how black judges, as members of an ethnic minority, *should* behave.[74] Others have only touched on judicial race tangentially as minor parts of larger investigations.[75]

Limited discussion also results from the obviously limited experiences of blacks as political decisionmakers. Much to their chagrin, blacks frequently find authority inversely related to their ability to secure a position. Baron rarely observed blacks in positions of ultimate control in his Chicago study and claims that it is precisely because blacks do not participate in key policy decisions that the status quo remains in housing, education, and employment.[76] If the illusion of power is all that exists for many black elites,[77] there is no decisional record to be examined.

Black trial judges may be the handful of exceptions to this general pattern. They bear the ultimate responsibility to see that justice is done in their courts; they evaluate proper practice and procedure, balance conflicting demands for due process and efficiency, and are held accountable for their decisions upon appellate review. Therefore, not only does chapter 4 present the first systematic examination of black judicial behavior, but it may also be the most comprehensive study of black political decision making generally.

What might we expect to find? Some social scientists feel that behavioral differences between black and white judges should be anticipated. Parenti claims that as long as ethnic differences exist, "... ethnic-oriented responses will be found even among those who have made a 'secure' professional and social position for themselves...."[78] Nagel expects this sweeping hypothesis will hold for judges; ethnic differences are associated with different value orientations which, in turn, should be manifest in different decisional tendencies.[79] Support for a race-sentencing relationship can also be found in the more general belief that the sentencing tendencies of judges may well be determined before they rise to the bench. According to Sheldon and Eleanor Glueck, "... what determines whether a judge will be severe or lenient is to be found in the environment to which the judge has been subjected previous to his becoming an administrator of sentences."[80] Given the fact that blackness has been a badge of inferiority, deprivation, and persecution, their common racial identity may also describe a range of experiences and beliefs shared by black jurists. Finally, the special circumstances that still attend the black judicial presence, including self-perceived roles as educators and reformers, might result in measurable behavioral differences.

Complicating matters are some reasonable arguments that few race-related disparities will appear. First, much of the work linking judicial background to behavior has focused on appellate judges, and even here the significance of the relationships has been challenged.[81] Second, the strength of the processes of legal and judicial socialization may lessen, if not virtually eliminate, the systematic impact of shared experiential or other background characteristics.[82] Third, evidence of extraordinary institutional and environmental pressures on black jurists to conform, including scrutiny by public officials and the news media, might also lessen the likelihood that marked differences in behavior will emerge.[83] Finally, the observations of reporters investigating the black legal community in Washington, D.C. included an assessment that black judges' approaches to crime and punishment varied widely.[84] If it is confirmed by actual dispositional data, individuality rather than racial conformity would be the most accurate characterization of the black judiciary.

To determine which set of propositions is supported in Metro City, first we examine the tendency of black judges to favor the defense or prosecution in various types of felony cases and then we compare their decisions to those handed down by white judges. Verdicts in bench trial cases and sentence lengths for all offenders are contrasted by racial group and the individual trial judge. The results of this analysis indicate with considerable specificity whether black jurists are more or less lenient than their white colleagues or whether individual factors rather than racial identity per se are more important in trial court decision making. Next, we can investigate differences in inter- and intraracial defendant treatment by determining whether decisional tendencies systematically differ when the defendant is a member of the judge's own rather than another racial group. This aspect of the inquiry provides tangible evidence whether black, or for that matter white, judges play racial favorites—information that is central to arguments both for and against an expanded black recruitment effort.

By looking at treatment accorded black and white defendants, we begin to shift attention to the external or output side of the race question. Chapter 5 focuses on the subject of possible discriminatory defendant treatment exclusively. Unlike investigating black judicial performance, there is a considerable body of research to guide this exploration. Unfortunately, much of it is contradictory. Some scholars charge blatant prejudicial treatment against black defendants; others attribute race-related disparities to class-based systemic inequities that place blacks at a greater disadvantage than whites. And still others believe that greater black criminality, such as more extensive prior criminal records, explains what might appear at first glance to be harsher black sentencing.[85] This uncertainty, requests for additional research,[86] and a history of past racial discrimination acknowledged by all underlie this effort to first describe and then interpret race-related disparities in the treatment of Metro City felony offenders.

Comparisons between black and white defendants are made within and across felony crime categories at the verdict and sentencing stages. In contrast to the judicial analysis, factors in addition to race, crime type, and disposition are incorporated because divergent explanations appear to have resulted, in part, from the complexity of the decisional process itself. A group of legal and extralegal factors may influence ultimate case outcome and also be associated with defendant race. If so, what appears as an absolute race-disposition disparity may be partly or entirely attributable to nonracial factors. For instance, defendants with court-appointed attorneys often fare worse in the dispositional process than do those with privately retained counsel; blacks also happen to be more likely to be represented by public defenders.[87] The direct effect of race on case outcome can and should be distinguished from the indirect effect resulting from this possible economic/systemic factor.

Competing explanations are formally developed in a causal model and then tested by using path analytic techniques. A complete elaboration is necessary initially because not every theoretically relevant variable is included in the Metro City data. Missing factors are identified first so the subsequent analysis will not disregard possible biasing influences. In addition to type of counsel, bail status, type of plea, charge severity, and charge reduction are included in the computerized case histories.

One black judge has written, "To deny that racism exists throughout our judicial system is to be oblivious to the most fundamental truth about 20th century America.... There is no equal justice for black people; there has never been."[88] Some have denied this charge while others have interpreted events differently. The primary purposes of chapter 5 are to clarify these contradictory perspectives and then evaluate them in the context of a major urban trial court.

The appropriateness of a trial courtroom setting in general and the suitability of the Metro City court in particular are critical to the success of this investigation. Trial courts are significant political and policy-making institutions. Verdicts and sentences are authoritatively allocated negative values to those who are convicted. More so than state appellate or federal tribunals, trial courts are responsible on a day-to-day basis for giving practical meaning to such lofty democratic ideals as justice and equality. They establish case-specific policy in resolving conflicts among individuals and between the individual and the state. And for all practical purposes, lower state courts are courts of both last resort and lasting impression for the vast majority of litigants.[89]

With such critical responsibilities, it is disturbing to discover that trial courts, if not failing, are at least falling far short of fulfilling their obligations to the defendant and the community. Inadequate financial resources and overcrowded dockets mean that speed and efficiency are overemphasized, the presumption of innocence is underemphasized, and impersonality and insensitivity pervade nearly all legal proceedings. In most jurisdictions, mammoth backlogs resulting in unconscionable periods of delay make prompt case disposition of all civil and many criminal matters impossible. While serious, these problems do not necessarily overshadow race as a cause of concern. Trial courts may, in fact, be the most important legal arena today in which to examine racial issues. According to Judge Crockett, "The battleground today is the trial courts... and especially the lowest trial courts. It is in these tribunals that legally approved racism-classism flourishes in its most virulent form."[90]

The problems confronting the trial court in Metro City paint a familiar picture of urban court ills. The blanket charge has been made that this court does not dispense justice.[91] Wide sentence disparities have been reported amid a continuing controversy over the quality of judicial performance. Mixed reports come from studies dealing in part at least with racial variables. One project concluded that defendant race had no impact on case outcome; a subsequent study found some relationship while the most recent concluded that discriminatory treatment was commonplace.

This uncertainty alone makes the research setting attractive. In addition, the sixteen black jurists on the bench represent a significant portion of the still meager national total. They are given wide discretionary sentencing powers to deal with a large defendant population that is 80 percent black. In investigating the race issue in the Metro City trial court, we are examining questions of utmost importance to the just administration of our laws in a legal arena wholly appropriate for their examination. We can begin by discussing Metro City, its trial court, and the trial court data.

Notes

1. Gunnar Myrdal, *An American Dilemma* (New York: Harper & Brothers, 1944).

2. Southern Regional Council, *Race Makes the Difference: An Analysis of Sentence Disparity among Black and White Offenders in Southern Prisons* (Atlanta: Southern Regional Council, 1969).

3. A. Leon Higgenbotham, *From the Outside Looking In: Is Yesterday's*

Racism Relevant to Today's Corrections? (Washington: Law Enforcement Assistance Administration, 1970); Robert M. Regoli and Donnell E. Jerome, "Recruitment of a Minority Group into an Established Institution: The Police," *Journal of Police Science and Administration* 3 (December 1975):410-416; Basil A. Paterson, "Blacks and the Justice System," in *From the Black Bar,* ed. Gilbert Ware (New York: G.P. Putnam's Sons, 1976), pp. 184-190.

4. For a discussion of black legal underrepresentation generally, see Walter J. Leonard, "The Development of the Black Bar," *Annals of the American Academy of Political and Social Science* 407 (May 1973):134-143; Kellis E. Parker and Betty J. Stebman, "Legal Education for Blacks," *Annals of the American Academy of Political and Social Science* 407 (May 1973):144-156.

5. Quoted in Parker and Stebman, "Legal Education for Blacks," p. 147.

6. Ware, *From the Black Bar;* Ernest Gellhorn, "The Law Schools and the Negro," *Duke Law Journal* (December 1968):1069-1097; Sar A. Levitan et al., *Still a Dream: The Changing Status of Blacks since 1960* (Cambridge, Mass.: Harvard University Press, 1975); Kenneth Tollett, "Black Lawyers, Their Education and the Black Community," *Howard Law Journal* 17 (1972):326-357.

7. These figures probably underestimate the actual disparity because proportionately more black attorneys serve a predominantly white clientele than vice versa.

8. George Crockett, "Commentary: Black Judges and the Black Judicial Experience," *Wayne Law Review* 19 (November 1972):61-71.

9. See Lucius J. Barker and Jesse J. McCorry Jr., *Black Americans and the Political System* (Cambridge, Mass.: Winthrop Publishers, 1976); "The Black Judge in America," *Judicature* 57 (June/July 1973):18-25; Lawrence Mosher, "Few Blacks Make the Bench," *National Observer,* December 1, 1969, p. 26.

10. Mosher, ibid.

11. Beverly Blair Cook, "Black Representation in the Third Branch," *Black Law Journal* 1 (Winter 1971):260-279.

12. For examples of these disturbing disparities, see Peter Blau and Otis Dudley Duncan, *The American Occupational Structure* (New York: John Wiley & Sons, Inc., 1967), p. 208, and Levitan et al., *Still a Dream.* Of course, educational deficiencies are not the only obstacles many black children confront that could affect chances of pursuing a higher education. Others such as poverty, the absence of a supportive home environment, or peer motivation also influence the acquisition of basic skills at a child's disposal.

13. Quoted in George Neff Stevens, "Bar Examinations and Minority Group Applicants," *American Bar Association Journal* 56 (October 1970):969-972.

14. Quoted in Christopher Edley, "The Black Lawyer and Institutional Employment," *Harvard Law School Bulletin* 22 (February 1971):46.

15. See, for example, John A. Winterbottom, "Light on the Law School

Admission Test," *Student Law Journal* 9 (October 1963):12-14, 30-32; Thomas M. Goolsby, "A Study of the Criteria for Legal Education and Admission to the Bar," *Journal of Legal Education* 20 (1967):175-195; Charles Consalus, "The Law School Admission Test and the Minority Student," *University of Toledo Law Review* (Spring/Summer 1970):501-524.

16. Gellhorn, "Law Schools and the Negro," p. 1073.

17. Harry T. Edwards, "A New Role for the Black Law Graduate—A Reality or an Illusion," *Michigan Law Review* 69 (1971):1409-1412; Alfred Blumrosen, "Legal Education for Black Students: A Remedy for Class Discrimination," *University of Toledo Law Review* (Spring/Summer 1970):800; Walter J. Leonard, "Forward: The Black Lawyer in America Today," *Harvard Law School Bulletin* 22 (February 1971):7.

18. Derrick Bell, "Black Students in White Law Schools: The Ordeal and the Opportunity," *University of Toledo Law Review* (Spring/Summer 1970):541-542; Henry McGee, "Black Lawyers and the Struggle for Racial Justice in the American Social Order," *Buffalo Law Review* 20 (Fall 1970):426; Jerome Shuman, "A Black Lawyers Study," *Howard Law Journal* 16 (Winter 1971):230-231.

19. Shuman, ibid., pp. 233, 274.

20. Parker and Stebman, "Legal Education for Blacks," pp. 148-151.

21. Shuman, "A Black Lawyers Study," p. 233.

22. Earl Carl, "The Shortage of Negro Lawyers: Pluralistic Negro Education and Legal Services for the Poor," *Journal of Legal Education* 20 (1967):21.

23. Maynard Jackson, "The Black American and the Legal Profession: A Study in Commitment," *Journal of Public Law* 20 (1971):379.

24. Haywood Burns, "Racism and American Law: A New Course in Legal History," *University of Toledo Law Review* (Spring/Summer 1970):903-912; Gellhorn, "Law Schools and the Negro," pp. 1076-1077.

25. Bell, "Black Students in White Law Schools," p. 548.

26. Ibid., pp. 544-545.

27. Ibid.; Derrick Bell, "The Black Lawyer in Legal Education," *Harvard Law School Bulletin* 22 (February 1971):26; Eugene L. Meyer and Joseph D. Whitaker, "Black Attorneys at Law," *The Washington Post,* April 14, 1976, pp. A1, A8.

28. Charles L. Mitchell, "The Black Philadelphia Lawyer," *Villanova Law Review* 20 (1974/1975):381; Parker and Stebman, "Legal Education for Blacks," pp. 148-151; Meyer and Whitaker, "Black Attorneys at Law," *The Washington Post,* April 11, 1976, p. A18.

29. Shuman, "A Black Lawyers Study," p. 230; O.T. Wells, "The Black Lawyer in Private Practice," *Harvard Law School Bulletin* 22 (February 1971):8-9; Leonard, "The Development of the Black Bar," p. 140.

30. Mitchell, "The Black Philadelphia Lawyer," pp. 387-389.

31. Robert O'Neil, "Preferential Admissions: Equalizing Access to Legal

Education," *University of Toledo Law Review* (Spring/Summer 1970): 298; Jackson, "The Black American and the Legal Profession," p. 380.

32. Jackson, ibid., p. 379.

33. Crockett, "Commentary," p. 62.

34. George Crockett, "Racism in the Courts," *Journal of Public Law* 20 (1971):388-389.

35. See, for example, Richard Kluger, *Simple Justice* (New York: Alfred A. Knopf, Inc., 1976).

36. Myrdal, *An American Dilemma*, p. 325.

37. James D. Montgomery, "The Black Lawyer and the Human and Civil Rights Struggle," *Harvard Law School Bulletin* 22 (February 1971):22.

38. McGee, "Black Lawyers and the Struggle for Racial Justice," pp. 428-429; Michael Katz, "Black Law Students in White Law Schools: Law in a Changing Society," *University of Toledo Law Review* (Spring/Summer 1970):590-591; Abram Kardiner and Lionel Ovesey, *The Mark of Oppression* (New York: The World Publishing Company, 1966), pp. 302-303.

39. Mosher, "Few Blacks Make the Bench," p. 26.

40. Joseph C. Howard, "Why We Organize," *Journal of Public Law* 20 (1971):381-382. See also Robert L. Evans, "The Black Lawyer and the Judiciary," *Harvard Law School Bulletin* 22 (February 1971):33 and George Crockett, "The Role of the Black Judge," *Journal of Public Law* 20 (1971):398.

41. A. Leon Higgenbotham, "The Black Lawyer in America Today," *Harvard Law School Bulletin* 22 (February 1971):57.

42. For example, Judge Robert Evans says, "So far as black judges are concerned, those of us who have had ghetto backgrounds can easily spot some of the factors that cause people to go into crime." Evans, "The Black Lawyer and the Judiciary," p. 34. See also Warner Smith, "George W. Crockett: The Opener-Interview," *The Black Law Journal* 1 (Winter 1971):258; Barker and McCorry, *Black Americans and the Political System*, p. 158.

43. Crockett, "The Role of the Black Judge," p. 398.

44. George Crockett, "A Black Judge Speaks," *Judicature* 53 (April/May 1970):365.

45. Quoted in Smith, "George W. Crockett," p. 258.

46. Howard, "Why We Organize"; Bell, "The Black Lawyer in Legal Education," p. 25; Smith, "George W. Crockett," p. 259.

47. Evans, "The Black Lawyer and the Judiciary," p. 32. See also Mitchell, "The Black Philadelphia Lawyer," p. 389.

48. J. Otis Cochran, "Some Thoughts on American Law Schools, the Legal Profession, and the Role of Students," *University of Toledo Law Review* (Spring/Summer 1970):623-631; William H. Brown, "Racial Discrimination in the Legal Profession," *Judicature* 53 (April/May 1970):385-389.

49. Crockett, "The Role of the Black Judge," p. 400.

50. Gordon Allport, *The Nature of Prejudice* (New York: Doubleday and

Company, 1958), pp. 261-263; Barbara Kruger MacKenzie, "The Importance of Contact in Determining Attitudes toward Negroes," *The Journal of Abnormal and Social Psychology* 43 (January 1948):417.

51. McGee, "Black Lawyers and the Struggle for Racial Justice," p. 428.

52. The subsequent historical discussion relies heavily on the compelling analyses of Tollett and Burns and the sources cited therein. See Kenneth Tollett, "Blacks, Higher Education and Integration," *Notre Dame Lawyer* 48 (October 1972):189-207 and Haywood Burns, "Black People and the Tyranny of American Law," *Annals of the American Academy of Political and Social Science* 407 (May 1973):156-166.

53. See the U.S. Constitution, Art. 1, secs. 2 and 9; Art. 4, sec. 2; and also see generally A. Leon Higgenbotham, *In a Matter of Color* (New York: Oxford University Press, 1978).

54. *Scott* v. *Sanford,* 60 U.S. (19 How.) 393 (1857).

55. Higgenbotham, "The Black Lawyer in America Today," pp. 56-57.

56. *Bylew* v. *U.S.* 80 (13 Wall.) 581 (1871); *Civil Rights Cases* 109 U.S. 3 (1883).

57. 163 U.S. 537 (1896).

58. Quoted in Crockett, "A Black Judge Speaks," p. 361.

59. See, for example, James Eisenstein and Herbert Jacob, *Felony Justice* (Boston: Little, Brown and Company, 1977); John Hagan, "Extra-Legal Attributes and Criminal Sentencing: An Assessment of a Sociological Viewpoint," *Law and Society Review* 8 (Spring 1974):357-383; and the discussion in chapter 5.

60. Burns, "Racism and American Law," p. 911.

61. Representative research is Leo Carroll and Margaret E. Mondrick, "Racial Bias in the Decision to Grant Parole," *Law and Society Review* 11 (Fall 1976):93-107; David M. Petersen and Paul C. Friday, "Early Release from Incarceration: Race as a Factor in the Use of 'Shock Probation,' " *The Journal of Criminal Law and Criminology* 66 (March 1975):79-87; Marvin E. Wolfgang and Marc Reidel, "Race, Judicial Discretion and the Death Penalty," *Annals of the American Academy of Political and Social Science* 407 (May 1973):119-133.

62. Gilbert Ware, "Auction Block Justice," *Focus* 2 (July 1974):4-5; Crockett, "A Black Judge Speaks," p. 361.

63. Henry Allen Bullock, "Significance of the Racial Factor in the Length of Prison Sentences," *Journal of Criminal Law, Criminology and Police Science* 52 (November/December 1961):411-417. See also Edward F. Bell, "The Black Lawyer and the Judiciary," *Harvard Law School Bulletin* 22 (February 1971):31-35 and Ware, *From the Black Bar,* p. xxiv.

64. Derrick Bell, "Racism in American Courts: Cause for Black Disruption or Despair?" *California Law Review* 62 (January 1973):183-184.

65. William J. Chambliss, *Crime and the Legal Process* (New York: McGraw-Hill Book Company, 1969), p. 294.

66. Ibid.; Daniel H. Swett, "Cultural Bias in the American Legal System," *Law and Society Review* 4 (August 1969):100.

67. Howard Moore and Jane Bond Moore, "Some Reflections on the Criminal Justice System," in *From the Black Bar,* ed. Ware, p. 34; Austin Turk, *Criminality and the Legal Order* (Chicago: Rand McNally & Company, 1972), pp. 53-78.

68. Edward Brooke, "Introduction to the Symposium," *University of Toledo Law Review* (Spring/Summer 1970):277-279; O'Neil, "Preferential Admissions."

69. The President's Crime Commission, *Task Force Report: The Courts* (Washington: Government Printing Office, 1967), p. 50.

70. This assumes, of course, that black legal professionals will generally be able to identify with black litigants more closely given their common racial bond; this assumption is challenged by those who contend that the black legal elite will itself be predominantly middle-class in background and values.

71. Marvin Wolfgang, *Crime and Race* (New York: Institute of Human Relations Press, 1964), p. 45; Chambliss, *Crime and the Legal Process,* p. 292; Milton D. Morris, *The Politics of Black America* (New York: Harper & Row, Publishers, 1975), p. 3.

72. See Harold M. Baron, "Black Powerlessness in Chicago," *Transaction* 6 (November 1968):27-33; Crockett, "The Role of the Black Judge"; "The Black Judge in America."

73. S.J. Makielski, *Beleaguered Minorities* (San Francisco: W.H. Freeman and Company, 1973), p. 131.

74. Stuart Nagel, "Ethnic Affiliations and Judicial Propensities," *Journal of Politics* 24 (February 1962):92-110.

75. Charles Engle, "Criminal Justice in the City: A Study of Sentence Severity and Variation in the Philadelphia Court System," Ph.D. dissertation, Temple University, 1971; Donald Bartlett and James Steele, "Crime and Injustice," *Philadelphia Inquirer,* February 18-24, 1973.

76. Baron, "Black Powerlessness in Chicago."

77. For other examples see Alvin Poussaint, "Black Administrators in the White University," *Black Scholar* 6 (September 1974):8-14; Wilbur Rich, "Special Role and Role Expectation of Black Administrators of Neighborhood Mental Health Programs," *Community Mental Health Journal* 11 (Winter 1975):394-401.

78. Michael Parenti, "Ethnic Politics and the Persistence of Ethnic Identification," *American Political Science Review* 61 (September 1967):724.

79. Nagel, "Ethnic Affiliations and Judicial Propensities," p. 110.

80. Sheldon Glueck and Eleanor Glueck, *Ventures in Criminology* (Cambridge, Mass.: Harvard University Press, 1964), p. 180.

81. Henry Glick and Kenneth Vines, *State Court Systems* (Englewood Cliffs, N.J.: Prentice-Hall, Inc., 1973), p. 77; Joel Grossman, "Social Backgrounds and Judicial Decision-Making," *Harvard Law Review* 79 (June 1966):1551-1564; S. Sidney Ulmer, "Dissent Behavior and the Social Backgrounds of Supreme Court Justices," *Journal of Politics* 32 (August 1970):584.

82. Robert Traynor, "Who Can Best Judge the Judges," *Virginia Law Review* 53 (October 1967):1271; Kenneth Vines, "The Judicial Role in American States," in *The Frontiers of Judicial Research*, eds. Joel Grossman and Joseph Tanenhaus (New York: John Wiley & Sons, Inc., 1969), pp. 461-485.

83. Crockett, "A Black Judge Speaks," pp. 363-364; Bell, "The Black Lawyer and the Judiciary," p. 31.

84. Meyer and Whitaker, "Black Attorneys at Law," *The Washington Post*, April 15, 1976, p. 14.

85. See the discussion in chapter 5.

86. Wolfgang, *Crime and Race*, p. 45; Chambliss, *Crime and the Legal Process*, p. 292.

87. David Sudnow, "Normal Crimes: Sociological Features of the Penal Code in a Public Defender's Office," in *Crime and Justice in Society*, ed. Richard Quinney (Boston: Little, Brown and Company, 1969), p. 321; Stuart Nagel, "The Tipped Scales of American Justice," in *The Politics of Local Justice*, eds. James Klonoski and Robert Mendelsohn (Boston: Little, Brown and Company, 1970), p. 121.

88. Crockett, "A Black Judge Speaks," p. 361.

89. Glick and Vines, *State Court Systems*, p. 5; Raymond Bauer, "The Study of Policy Formation: An Introduction," in *The Study of Policy Formation*, eds. Raymond Bauer and Kenneth Gergen (New York: The Free Press, 1968), p. 3; Julian D'Esposito, "Sentencing Disparities: Causes and Cures," *The Journal of Criminal Law, Criminology and Police Science* 60 (June 1969): 183; Charles Stafford, "The Public's View of the Judicial Role," *Judicature* 52 (August/September 1968):73.

90. Crockett, "Racism in the Courts," p. 387.

91. Information that could reveal either Metro City or its court is omitted to maintain anonymity that was guaranteed in all written work as a precondition to utilizing the data examined here. Please contact the author directly for additional background material.

2 Metro City, Its Court, and the Trial Court Data

Metro City—Demographics and Politics[1]

State trial courts are heavily influenced by the communities they serve. To understand the politics of race in the courts, it becomes necessary to understand some of the basic demographic and political characteristics of the city. Metro City, a large, Northeastern urban center, has had a relatively stable center-city population of about 2 million since 1920. This overall stability, however, disguises marked changes in the population mix that have taken place in recent years. In 1940 blacks comprised 13 percent of the city's residents. By 1970 that figure had reached 33 percent, and a total black population in excess of 0.5 million was fourth nationally. In the postwar period, three predominantly black ghettos developed, and the public schools, segregated until 1959, began to enroll a majority of black students.

Black in-migration and higher birthrates were largely offset by the movement of white middle- and upper-class city dwellers to nearby suburbs. Remaining in substantial numbers throughout the period were lower-income whites, often of first- or second-generation foreign stock. Today, in addition to its sizable black population, center-city residents can be roughly grouped as follows: Catholics, mainly of Irish and Italian descent, 30 percent; Jews, frequently of Russian descent, 13 percent; and Protestants of diverse national origins, 18 percent.

The Metro City economy has also undergone recent change as the city slowly shifted from manufacturing to nonmanufacturing enterprise. Nearly 50,000 jobs were lost as textile, petroleum, clothing, and other heavy industry operations were curtailed. Nonmanufacturing employment took up only part of the slack, and the city as a whole has fared poorly in competition for corporate headquarters with its Northeastern corridor neighbors. Total employment decline in the city proper has exceeded 100,000.

The recent political history of Metro City centers on the struggles between reform elements within the community and first a Republican and then a Democratic party machine. Prior to the New Deal, the city went overwhelmingly Republican in most elections. For example, the mayoral candidate in 1931 received 90 percent of the vote. During the 1930s and 1940s, national and statewide elections were more closely contested, but throughout the period a strong Republican party organization continued to control the municipal government.

Widespread charges of corruption and bossism leveled against the Republican organization contributed to the eventual success of a reform movement. Running under the Democratic banner, the reformers captured the mayor's office in the early 1950s and launched pioneering urban renewal and downtown renovation programs in addition to expanding job opportunities for minorities. At the heart of this public-regarding urban coalition of reformers were the business and civic elites, moderates and progressives from both political parties, middle- and upper-class city residents, and university activists.

A patronage and power-hungry Democratic organization was reluctant to cooperate with the reformers; and by the end of the decade, reform and organization Democrats were feuding openly. The organization achieved the upper hand in 1963 with the election of a Democratic ward leader as mayor. Since that time, the string of Democratic organization victories has remained unbroken. Recent leadership in the city can be characterized as narrowly partisan and highly pragmatic. Power is centralized while patronage is keyed to past loyalty and the expectation of future support. The electoral coalition that dominates the city today depends on the allegiance of organized labor, lower- and middle-class white ethnics, blacks, and an extensive civil service bureaucracy (teachers, police officers, fire fighters). The city remains solidly Democratic as evidenced by a 2.5 to 1 voter registration advantage and a 56 percent majority given George McGovern in his ill-fated 1972 Presidential bid.

The black experience in Metro City has been bittersweet at best. Concern for human rights holds a distinguished place in the city's history, yet promises often outstripped performance as far as actual opportunities for blacks were concerned. Traditional black political loyalty to the Republican party began to fade with the coming of the New Deal, and the overwhelming (more than 80 percent) black support for the Democratic ticket that was essential for the reform victory in 1952 has been maintained subsequently. The reform era meant more than empty promises for blacks. Through the stricter enforcement of civil service regulations, blacks were able to secure a substantial number of jobs in the public sector for the first time; a human relations commission was established, in part, to eliminate discriminatory employment practices in the private sector; and a civilian police review board became a symbol of the reform mayor's concern for the rights of the poor and politically powerless.

Although these changes signaled progress, race-related inequities remained large. For example, although blacks had achieved proportional representation in the city workforce by 1963, they held fewer than 1 percent of the positions paying more than $7,000 annually. Blacks fared no better as the result of subsequent organization victories. They received a share of the patronage, but their rewards were generally less substantial than their contribution to election victories.

Several explanations have been offered to account for the relatively weak political position of blacks in Metro City. First, the absence of a black political machine required that successful black politicians become dependent, to some extent, on the white-dominated political organizations. Second, blacks did not participate in city politics as a cohesive and unified force. At times, black groups and individuals competed among themselves for power, thus weakening their collective influence. Political favors have often been dispensed to black leaders individually by machine politicians who see it in their best interest to maintain this fragmentation.

Third, black politicians themselves have not been particularly race-conscious. Appearing primarily interested in their own advancement, many acted as if their first responsibility was to the party organization rather than to a larger black constituency in the city. Racial considerations were also minimized in political campaigns. Election appeals by blacks to blacks often avoided both special pleas for racial solidarity and campaign promises of primary benefit to the black community. Finally, black participation in nearly all forms and levels of politics (registration, voting, party activity, office holding) has been less than comparable activity by whites. Black withdrawal or nonparticipation was often rational given the absence of viable alternatives to machine candidates. But the results were an inability to maximize political influence and little incentive for white politicians to address specifically the needs of the black community. Recent events and election returns indicate increasing black dissatisfaction with their traditional subservient role, perhaps foreshadowing greater voting independence and the creation of a potent third force in city politics. But in the past and for the moment, the black politician and voter alike remain dependent on white-dominated political organizations.

This political weakness has undoubtedly hampered efforts to close the gaps that exist between the city's black and white residents with regard to various quality-of-life indicators. The black unemployment rate has consistently been about twice that of whites; the same ratio exists for infant mortality. Whites in the city are still twice as likely to have some college experience and four times as likely to have graduated. Their median income is over 50 percent greater than blacks' median income, and their chances of pursuing a professional career are twice those of blacks.

Compared to figures for the black population nationally, however, Metro City blacks are above average. In 1970 the median number of school years completed by Metro City blacks was 10.4, with an accompanying high school graduation rate of 33.3 percent. For the entire country, the median school years completed was 9.8 with 31.4 percent of the black students graduating. The percentage of blacks living below the poverty line in Metro City (24.9 percent) was substantially below the figure for black Americans nationally (34.8 percent). Also encouraging has been the sustained growth of the black middle-class within the city. During the 1960s, black families with annual incomes in excess of $10,000 increased by more than 650 percent, and by the end of the decade they constituted nearly one-third of all black families in the city.

Crime and the Court

There are about 250,000 crimes reported in Metro City each year, with burglary and automobile theft comprising over half of the major offenses. Crime rates are more comparable to large cities nationwide than to most communities in the state. Federal Bureau of Investigation data show Metro City ranking near the bottom of fifteen large cities in the occurrence of the seven so-called Index crimes.[2] Its per capita property crime rate (burglary, larceny, automobile theft) was last while violent crimes (homicide, rape, robbery, aggravated assault) ranked tenth. Changes in these averages followed the national trend during the period studied, but the swings appeared less sharp than elsewhere. For example, the crime rates in New York City, Detroit, and San Francisco fell by more than 10 percent in 1972 while Metro City's decreased by less than 5 percent.

Metro City may do fairly well apprehending the perpetrators of crimes. The city's clearance rate for 1971 was 36.8 percent, almost double the national average that year. Probable offenders were arrested more often than the national norm in every Index category. The police chief was quick to take credit for these figures, citing effective patrol operations, investigative units, and citizen cooperation. Critics, however, questioned the accuracy of police reporting methods and pointed to unsolved crimes (63 percent) as evidence that there was still plenty of room for improvement.

Those who have the misfortune of being arrested in this city are unceremoniously channeled into the court system. The Metro City court comprises the state's largest judicial district and is one of fifty-nine courts of original jurisdiction in the state. Most trial court appeals are heard by a seven-member appellate court which has jurisdiction over all criminal convictions other than felonious murder. Jurisdiction in murder appeals resides in the state supreme court which also hears criminal and civil matters if requested to do so by two of its seven justices.

The court structure in Metro City is more complex than in the rest of the state, with the judicial district consisting of two courts instead of one. The primary trial court of general jurisdiction (the setting of this inquiry) shares a limited portion of its docket with a lower-level arraignment court. The arraignment court hears criminal cases carrying a potential maximum sentence of five years or less, civil cases when no more than $500 is involved, landlord-tenant controversies, and code enforcement proceedings.[3] Litigants do not have the right to a jury trial in this court, so they may appeal to the trial court where de novo proceedings with a jury are guaranteed; in 1972 the appeal rate from the arraignment court was 17 percent. This court also conducts preliminary hearings for felonies later heard in the trial court. A dismissal is required if a prima facie case against a defendant cannot be established by the state. Thus, by trying some cases and dismissing others, the arraignment court serves as a screening mechanism for the city's trial court.

The trial court itself consists of three divisions. A children's division hears cases involving juveniles, adoptions, and domestic relations while the estates court handles wills, trusts, estates, and the cases of incompetents. The bulk of both civil and criminal matters is disposed of in the court's trial division, however. Approximately 40,000 criminal cases enter the court system each year; 40 percent are dismissed at preliminary hearings, 25 percent are decided on their merits in the arraignment court, and the remaining 35 percent in addition to arraignment court appeals are heard in the trial court. Except for judicial salaries, the courts are funded by the city at a cost in excess of $20 million annually (7 percent of the city budget). At present more than 2,300 people are employed in court-related jobs.

The felony cases studied here have gone through several steps before reaching the trial court. Following arrest, the defendant is taken to the police administration building for preliminary arraignment. After being booked, fingerprinted, and photographed, the accused offender is interviewed to determine eligibility for one of several pretrial release options and/or court-appointed counsel. A formal presentation of charges also takes place; bail is set; a date for preliminary hearing is fixed or, if jurisdiction falls to the arraignment court, a trial date is established. Usually, the preliminary hearing is scheduled three days after the initial arraignment. These proceedings (also in the arraignment court) determine probable cause initially and are attended by the defendant, his or her attorney, an assistant district attorney, the arresting officer(s), witnesses, and a judge. If a prima facie case can be established, the defendant is then scheduled for a grand jury hearing in approximately two weeks. The grand jury essentially duplicates the function of the preliminary hearing by deciding whether there is probable cause that a crime was committed and that the defendant charged committed it.[4]

Shortly after grand jury proceedings conclude, the defendant is arraigned in the trial court. A trial date is set, and defense counsel appears on the record. The actual trial commences after pretrial motions are decided. Any defendant accused of a felony other than first-degree murder may waive a jury trial and be tried before a judge only. The judge then decides questions of law and fact and renders both a verdict and sentence. In jury trials, the twelve-member panel decides issues of fact while the judge rules on matters of law. During the trial, the defendant is represented by privately retained counsel or a court-appointed public or private defender.

Sentences are imposed with or without the benefit of a presentence report by a judge who, except in rare circumstances, was the presiding trial judge.[5] Occasionally posttrial motions are filed alleging errors in trial proceedings or challenging the sufficiency of evidence. These motions often are the basis for an appeal to a higher state court. After appeals are exhausted and the verdict and sentence stand, a convicted offender is sent to a county correctional institution if the maximum sentence is less than two years or to a state prison if it is greater than two years.

Sentences in felony cases are imposed by fifty-five trial division judges.

Together with twenty children's and six estates division jurists, they comprise the board of judges for trial court. Each judge is paid $40,000 a year to serve a ten-year term of office. The twenty-two arraignment court judges serve six-year terms at salaries of $35,000. The method of selection for both trial and arraignment judges has appointive and elective features. The governor temporarily fills a vacancy caused by retirement or death via appointment. These appointments require state senate confirmation unless the opening occurred while the legislature was adjourned. If an appointed judge wants to remain on the bench or an individual wants to seek initial judicial office, he must be elected. For the first ten-year term, successful candidates must win their party's endorsement, run under a party banner, and secure a plurality of the popular vote in the general election. Subsequently, judges seek reelection on a nonpartisan retention ballot where voters either approve or disapprove of their performance.

This textbook description does not do justice to the emotionally charged partisan atmosphere that usually surrounds judicial selection in Metro City. In a recent campaign, a conservative, "law and order" mayor urged the defeat of several judges seeking election after interim appointments, charging they were too lenient. The district attorney published a separate "hit list" while the Americans for Democratic Action defended those attacked. At the same time, two ostensibly impartial groups, the Good Judges for Metro City and the Metro City Bar Association, backed entire slates of candidates, first in the primary and then in the general election. While these battles were being fought, newspapers were editorializing their preferences and, most importantly, the two political parties were picking their own candidates. The outcome of this particular campaign was a resounding victory for candidates backed by the Democratic party, but it was a victory achieved after literally months of trading charges and countercharges about who was more, or usually less, qualified to sit on the Metro City bench.

An equally intense controversy had erupted a few years earlier when the governor appointed twenty-five judges to fill newly created seats on the trial bench while the legislature was adjourned. His choices allegedly represented rewards for past favors to various political leaders. Charges of favoritism were coupled with criticism over the judicial qualifications of those chosen. An aide to the governor offered a weak defense by saying, "At least they aren't *all* bums."[6] The highly partisan nature of these midnight appointments represented somewhat of a departure from the merit selection practices of previous governors. The fact these interim appointments were ending and full terms were at stake for such a large proportion of the bench undoubtedly added to the intensity of the election battle that was to follow.

Controversy over judicial appointments is only one aspect of the general politicization of the Metro City courts. Like its counterparts elsewhere, the trial court has taken the brunt of the criticism over the failure of the criminal justice system to "solve" the crime problem in the community. Headline stories and lead editorials in every city newspaper at one time or another have decried lenient sentences in notorious cases, charged individual judges with laxity bordering on incompetence, and noted that certain offenders and offender groups were not being punished harshly enough. The court has also served as a convenient scapegoat for the inabilities of others, more directly responsible for crime control, to deal with the crime problem satisfactorily. For example, the police commissioner went to great lengths to emphasize the large number of offenders arrested while on bail, probation, or parole. "If these fellows had been given the kind of sentence which the law permits and their prior crimes demanded, a substantial number of people in our city would not have been the victims of criminal acts."[7]

As a rule, judges are extremely reluctant to defend themselves publicly against such attacks. But perhaps indicative of the controversy that swirls about the court, the Metro City trial bench quickly came to its own defense. The board of judges issued an unjudicial statement saying it was "fed up with the rotten publicity judges were getting."[8] In more moderate tones, the chief judge carefully refuted negative statistical indicators of court performance, concluding that it defies logic to blame an increase in crime solely on the courts.

Political problems also developed within the court itself between 1968 and 1974. Patronage appointees accounted for 75 to 80 percent of the nonjudicial staff. Civil service rules did not apply, and job seekers were often given applications and told to return them along with letters from their respective ward leaders. The chief judge moved to institute a merit selection system and also establish an aptitude testing program to better match employee skills with job requirements. During this period, political control on the board of judges shifted from Republican to Democratic hands. Following this change, the Democrats were loathe to back reforms proposed by the now lame-duck Republican chief judge, and a confrontation was inevitable. The chief judge was partially victorious when several of his initiatives were supported by the state supreme court. Looking back at this period of turmoil, the chief judge, now in private practice, said with some feeling, "The board of judges is probably the only insane asylum run by its own inmates."[9]

Political problems were not the only matters troubling the court. Lengthy delays in criminal case disposition have plagued the system for years. In 1971 the average time from arrest to final disposition was just over 180 days. A three-month reduction was the goal of court officials, but the chances of near-term success appeared slim. The total number of untried felony cases carrying over from 1973 to 1974 was in excess of 4,700. The backlog problem on the civil side was even worse, with five- to seven-year delays in adjudication common and over 12,000 untried cases waiting to be heard. The addition of twenty-five judges was intended to attenuate, if not eliminate, the backlog problem. Unfortunately the new judges did neither.

Some observers say that an unusually large number of weak police arrests and a loose indictment policy by the district attorney's office are at the root of the backlog problem. The lack of an effective case screening mechanism is indicated by the fact that nearly 50 percent of all felony defendants are removed from the system before reaching the trial court. Several crimes have extremely high dismissal rates. Recently, 85 percent or more of the commercialized vice, liquor law, and gambling cases have been thrown out at preliminary hearings. Also indicative is a comparison between the Metro City and Chicago judiciaries. In 1971 there were over 19,000 indictments handed up in Metro City compared to 4,500 in Chicago and Cook County, an area with a larger population and higher crime rate.

An overburdened criminal justice system may also have contributed to two other characteristics of the Metro City court—relatively low conviction rates and few jury trials. Both the Metro City arraignment and trial courts produced proportionately fewer cases resulting in convictions and guilty pleas than did comparable urban judiciaries. Cases heard in 1971 yielded guilty verdicts less than 63 percent of the time; the following year this figure had decreased to under 57 percent. At the same time, guilty verdicts were being returned in 70 percent of the cases in Detroit, 82 percent in Los Angeles, and 84 percent in Baltimore. Part of the disparity might have been due to the reluctance of the prosecutor to make extensive use of plea bargaining and to offer attractive "deals" when negotiations did take place.[10] The size of the docket alone might also reduce the number of cases that could be prosecuted to the fullest extent of the law. If many cases were also weak, it is not too surprising that the overall conviction rate in Metro City was comparatively low.

The number of jury trial dispositions in Metro City has been increasing since 1965. Between 1965 and 1970 there was nearly a threefold increase (77 to 218). In relative terms, however, this court still has a low overall jury trial disposition rate. Jury trials comprised 2 percent of the docket compared to 9 percent in Boston and Cleveland, 7 percent in Baltimore, and 5 percent in Chicago. Harsh sentencing judges preside over jury trials in order to discourage them—a fact that is widely known in and out of the court. Evidence shows that courtroom regulars are very perceptive: for comparable crimes, jury sentences are indeed much higher than sentences following bench trials or plea bargains. Limited resources may also encourage harsher sanctions regardless of individual judicial sentencing philosophies simply because the court would not be able to function with a greatly increased number of jury trials.[11]

Political turmoil, overcrowded dockets, and resource constraints do not present a complete picture of the Metro City court system, however. In addition to its problems, the court is characterized by a forward-looking attitude toward innovation and reform. Two experimental programs have been established, with their eventual goal being a sizable reduction in case backlog. In one, assistant district attorneys are stationed in selected district police stations on a 24-hour basis. Their job is to screen out cases unlikely to result in a conviction—most often those where the evidence is weak or police procedure questionable. In the other, a preindictment probation program removes some first offenders from the normal case flow. Selected defendants are given the option of waiving their speedy-trial rights and formal convictions in return for accepting an unrestricted probation for a stated period. If an individual is rearrested while on probation, the original prosecution resumes; if not, all charges are dropped and no criminal record is maintained. This program saves considerable court time while giving those most likely to be rehabilitated a second chance.

Significant bail reforms also occurred in Metro City. A 10 percent deposit bail program was established following a scandal where arraignment court judges were discovered taking kickbacks from local bondsmen. Today, a defendant can obtain pretrial release by depositing 10 percent of the bond's face value with the court and receive 90 percent of the money back if she or he appears at all court proceedings. In addition, the court has expanded its pretrial services division to permit more defendants to be released on their own recognizance. After being interviewed by court personnel about community ties, employment, and family responsibilities, defendants deemed good risks are released on their own signature. While not achieving all that was expected, both programs have made pretrial release opportunities less dependent on a person's financial status and the predelictions of a bondsman.[1,2]

Other reforms include increasing the jurisdiction of the arraignment court and abolishing the indicting grand jury, both intended to speed case disposition. Also new rules limit the reasons for granting continuances and the total number of continuances possible in a criminal case. On the agenda for the future, according to court administrators, are a more humane pretrial detention facility, legislation to reduce the number of jurors in some criminal trials, and summary disposition methods for posttrial motions.

In many specific respects, Metro City and its court are unique. Historical development, political, social, and economic environments, and legal rules and methods of operation all distinguish the research setting. Consequently, the generalizations from this research must be qualified and remain tentative. Nevertheless, contextual differences between this court and other urban judiciaries and the problems facing this court and those confronting courts elsewhere appear only to be differences in degree rather than in kind. Political controversy, judicial infighting, overcrowded dockets, court delay, and various reform efforts are characteristic of many, if not all, major urban trial courts. While the specifics are indeed unique to the community, the general problems and patterns are broadly descriptive of modern U.S. courts.

In one important respect, the single-site location is a distinct research advantage. Because judges and defendants are operating in and affected by common legal and community environments, significant factors that may affect judicial behavior and case disposition patterns when contrasted across jurisdictions are held constant here. Racial differences by both judge and defendant race can be more easily and accurately gauged because jurisdictional changes in, for example, sentencing options, judicial selection methods, or courtroom procedures do not appear. While ideally one would like to conduct similar inquiries in a number of courts, Metro City offers a representative location to examine the impact of race, utilizing an unusually rich data set made available by the chief judge and court administrator.

Trial Court Data

Information used in the subsequent analysis is derived from three primary sources: judicial autobiographies, case histories of felony defendants, and personal interviews. Biographical data are employed primarily in assessing judicial backgrounds and careers (chapter 3) while case histories are used to gauge black judges' behavior (chapter 4) and black defendant treatment (chapter 5). The impressions and opinions of key courtroom participants, gleaned from interviews, supplement more objective measures throughout the discussion. Together, these data comprise one of the most extensive and reliable collections of information on the judicial staffing and decision making in any trial court and certainly the most complete ever gathered to study questions of race.

Background data on sixteen black and seventy-nine white judges are derived primarily from autobiographical reports completed by the judges on precoded forms at the request of the court's public information officer. A few judges either neglected to return forms or failed to complete them in their entirety. In these instances, information was usually obtained from the state manual or through special inquiries initiated by the public information officer; missing data are rare. Only active members of the trial bench during the time that the sentencing data were gathered are included in the sample; visiting and semi-active/retired judges have been omitted. The likelihood of factual error is minimal since, for the most part, the judges' self-reports are utilized. Their statements were subsequently checked with a less complete but independent compilation of judicial background characteristics. Few discrepancies were found; and on verification, those that did emerge resulted from inaccuracies in the other data source.

Interviews were conducted with twenty-five court personnel at various times between 1975 and 1978. Although a concerted effort was made to contact individuals participating in all significant decision-making activities, the primary focus was on the trial bench. Six black judges and four white judges active in the six-year period of study, including the chief judge, were personally interviewed at length (½ hour to 1½ hours) and asked a series of questions about their own experiences and general observations on the court. In addition, court administrators (four), assistant district attorneys (three), public defenders (three), private criminal attorneys (two), a bar association official, and black community leaders (two) were interviewed, principally by telephone. Notes were taken during all discussions with additional comments written immediately afterward. The views expressed by these court participants may not be entirely representative because the sample of interviewees in each category is small and stratification was possible by categorical group only. However, this limitation is not serious given that this interview material is primarily intended to supplement more comprehensive biographical and sentencing data.

In late 1967 Metro City became the largest city in the country to completely computerize its criminal record-keeping system—a system that subsequently has been praised as a model for other jurisdictions. Several years later, a consortium of criminal justice research agencies recommended that this sophisticated system be used to greater advantage; at the time the valuable case and defendant data being gathered were employed only for bookkeeping purposes, to keep track of defendants' cases as they progressed through the system. Taking this suggestion seriously, the chief judge authorized the use of this information for research under the strict proviso that the names of the city, judges, and defendants remain anonymous. The data subsequently made available include all felony cases docketed and disposed of between July 1968 and June 1974.

Several samples were drawn from this population based on the presence or absence of information central to the overall objectives of the project and the specific race question being examined. Cases were excluded from all analyses if they failed to record one or more of the following: valid criminal charge, case disposition, and sentence codes; race of defendant; the maximum possible sentence for the principal charge in the case; and certain variables relating to the trial judge including, of course, race. Also omitted in most instances were defendants not charged with one of the sixteen most common felony offenses occurring in Metro City. The resulting samples of validly coded cases for the analysis of judicial behavior include verdicts in 24,100 bench trial cases and 30,350 cases where sentence was imposed following a conviction or guilty plea. In gauging defendant treatment, 43,602 cases disposed of via bench trials, jury trials, or guilty pleas are examined along with the sentences meted out to 32,731 black and white defendants found guilty in these deliberations. The basic core of cases in these analyses is the same as are the general criteria used to retain or remove cases from the final samples. Differences in sample size are due primarily to the disposition stage (verdict or sentence) and the race question (judge's behavior or defendant treatment) being examined.

Invalid charge codes included offenses falling outside the general classification of crime categories established by the court administrator's office. Of more importance were cases deleted because of problematic disposition codes. The criterion determining validity was whether a clear determination of guilt or innocence was rendered. Omitted were cases noll prossed, transferred, dropped on a technicality, dismissed by grand jury, routed through preindictment probation, and those containing apparent coding errors. Finally, cases that indicated unclear or invalid sentence codes (for example, sentences to mental institutions or a case where a not-guilty disposition also recorded a punishment) were also dropped.

For several reasons cases were removed because of inadequate information on defendant race. Initially, records failing to contain a race code were eliminated. Most of these data appeared in 1968, the year after the computerized record-keeping system was initiated and can be attributed to early mechanical and procedural flaws. Since the primary interests here are black/white differences, the inclusion of additional racial or ethnic factors adds unnecessary and undesired complexity to the analysis. Because of this potential problem and evidence that disposition patterns may vary between other ethnic groups and *both* black and white defendants, defendants coded in an unspecified "other" race category were also eliminated.[13]

A few cases were deleted if the legislated maximum sentence for the principal criminal charge lodged against each defendant was not obtained. This variable, along with the felony crime category, is important in controlling for the varying severity of different offenses. With this information, crime severity can be distinguished from race to contrast the influence of legal and extralegal factors on sentencing. Statutory maximum penalties for the vast majority of criminal charges appearing in the data file were obtained from the state bureau of criminal justice statistics and added to the case histories.

To alleviate backlog pressures, out-of-town judges occasionally presided in the Metro City trial court. As transients, they were not subject to the common socialization experiences, courtroom relationships, and community influences generally assumed to be held constant. For this reason, cases decided by these judges were omitted along with those ruled on by arraignment court judges or semiretired judges. A minimal degree of judicial activity was conservatively established as at least twenty-five bench trial verdicts and twenty-five sentences. This cutoff left ninety-one judges (sixteen black and seventy-five white) in the behavioral analysis compared to the ninety-five included in the background inquiry. The average workload for each judge in the sample is 264 bench trials [standard deviation (s.d.) = 278] and 334 sentencing decisions (s.d. = 321). Equalizing the judges' caseloads by weighting does not alter the substantive findings reported in chapter 4.

The composition of the trial bench changed during the 1968-1974 period. Judges retired, died, or were defeated for reelection. However, the number of full-time trial judges (fifty-five), marginal changes in patterns of criminal activity (types of cases and defendants), and a stable courtroom environment enable these judges to be treated as a single trial bench for the purposes of this analysis. Within broad jury or bench trial judicial groupings, cases were assigned to individual judges as their courtrooms became available. This assignment method made "shopping" by either the judge or the defendant difficult.

Most defendants are arraigned on one of sixteen common felony offenses:

murder; manslaughter; robbery; aggravated assault; minor assault; burglary; larceny; automobile larceny; stolen property; forgery-counterfeiting; rape or other serious sex offenses; drug offenses; weapons offenses; driving under the influence; gambling; and contributing to the delinquency of a minor. Grouping the separate criminal charges that appear in the data into these categories is based on the coding scheme adopted by the office of court administration, a scheme itself derived from state law. These crimes encompass a broad range of criminal behavior and include all Uniform Crime Report offenses.

Central to any analysis of case disposition are reliable and accurate data. A conservative sample selection process has resulted in a solid research base. The samples, in effect, are all cases with nonmissing, error-free data on key variables across a representative group of crimes. Cases that were omitted do not bias the resulting samples in any known way. In addition, the computerized data processing techniques adopted by the court increase confidence in these data. A uniform coding scheme was in use during the entire six-year period under investigation. Case records were checked, updated, and rechecked while a file was active, increasing the likelihood that mistakes were caught and corrected.

The result is a large collection of cases containing complete dispositional histories along with extensive trial judge and defendant information.[14] Of equal importance to this inquiry is the scope of the race data. A collection of over 34,000 case histories of black felony defendants far exceeds most previous efforts. A sample of sixteen black judges represents about 8 percent of the nation's black trial bench, and their behavior in nearly 6,000 cases allows for the first extensive examination of black judicial decision making.

Frequently, a single charge, disposition, and sentence had to be selected among several in multiple-charge cases. Prior research served as a general guide with three criteria selected to break successive ties.[15] The initial basis for charge selection was actual sentence severity. That is, in multiple-charge cases, if one charge carried a sentence more severe than any other, it represented the "crime" for that particular case. This charge was judged to be most representative of the actual punishment accorded a defendant. In some instances, however, a single sentence did not emerge from this procedure as most severe. Ties remained because not-guilty verdicts were rendered or several charges received equally severe sentences. In these situations, *among those charges with tied maximum sentences,* the charge carrying the most severe *potential maximum penalty* (as defined by statute) was selected. Maximum sentences were calculated from a list of standard offenses in Metro City and state.

At this point fewer than 5 percent of the cases remained tied on maximum sentence severity and maximum charge severity. Charges still tied were grouped into general crime categories and these categories ranked as to severity. Ties were broken by choosing the charge in the most serious category. Finally, random selection was used to select among a few charges that were now virtually indistinguishable—falling in the same general crime category, carrying the same maximum potential punishment, and accorded the same actual sentence.

Three frequently investigated case outcomes serve as primary dependent variables in the decisional analyses (chapters 4 and 5). The decision to convict marks a critical turning point for the defendant. Without belaboring the obvious, the added burden a person assumes with a criminal record will have a bearing on the rest of his or her life. A dichotomous measure of guilt or innocence is utilized that indicates percentage rates at which judges convict or defendants are convicted. In a sentencing analysis, two measures are desirable. There is a qualitative difference between nonprison sanctions (suspended sentence, probation, fine) and a jail term. This important distinction is measured by another dichotomous variable, jail/no jail.

A second indicator of sentence severity for those found guilty deemphasizes the breaking point between prison and nonimprisonment and instead taps more subtle differences along a broader continuum. Joining past theory and practice to the data at hand results in a detailed 93-point sentence severity scale that makes meaningful distinctions between and among degrees of deprivation of individual freedom and the varying severity of nonprison sanctions. The scale can be subdivided into the following general categories, in increasing order of severity: suspended sentences only; fines only; suspended sentences and fines; probated sentences and probated sentences and fines; and active jail sentences.[16] The complete scale is found in appendix A.

Suspended sentences (scale value 1) are considered the least serious form of punishment handed down by a court. Usually involving little or no supervision and rarely revoked, suspended sentences have been termed judicial warnings. Next in increasing order of severity stand five fine categories. Unlike suspended sentences, they carry with them a penalty resulting in deprivation, but the potential for actual punishment is considered less than for either probated or active jail sentences. The logical extension of both these major divisions is a set of scale values for cases disposed of with both suspended sentences and fines.

Probationary sentences are ranked next in severity (scale values 12 to 31). Occasionally treated as less or equally severe as fines and suspended sentences, they are generally operationalized as more severe than both. This relative positioning is due to the conditional nature of the sentence as well as the greater restrictions placed on the offender. Probationary sentences vary, making it appropriate to differentiate among them on the sentencing scale. Finally, to avoid an unnecessary loss of information, probated sentences alone are distinguished from sentences of a similar length that include a fine.

The final sixty-one scale values represent the active sentencing options available to Metro City judges. Severity rankings in this project, as in nearly every previous work, are keyed to the *minimum* sentence as the most reliable indicator of the actual period of imprisonment expected. But additional information is incorporated by making secondary differentiations based on *maximum* sentences included in a decision.

The potential pitfalls attending the adoption of this particular scale are similar to those developed previously. There is an inevitable degree of arbitrariness in the ranking scheme. We must assume that this factor and others possibly distorting the scale values are randomly distributed and not systematically related to the independent variables studied. Also, sentence severity as measured here is most precisely an ordinal scale. The index is, however, open to interval interpretations. With the expectation that the results will be roughly linear to the scale, we may take advantage of stronger interval statistical techniques. While some valid ordinal transformation of the scale might be possible, it would be unlikely to change the results significantly.[17] Since all but two of the ninety-three categories are used, judges evidently perceive and respond to the wide variety of sentencing possibilities.

After the significance of the race issue and the strength of the data are emphasized, a few caveats are in order before we turn our attention to an assessment of black judges' backgrounds and careers. It is undoubtedly true that by working in a single court within one community the influence of hard-to-measure variations in state legal systems and community environments is controlled. The tradeoff, however, is that no matter how representative a particular research setting is, relationships unique to the court and the community will become confounded with more general behavioral patterns in such a way that their effects cannot be disentangled. This problem arises frequently in judicial research, and there is no reason to think that Metro City and its trial court are any more or less idiosyncratic than other major U.S. cities and courts. Nevertheless, no matter how definitive our answers are here, it remains necessary to address these racial questions again in other legal arenas.

A true measure of any judicial system *qua* system must be based on an evaluation of an entire dispositional process—an assessment of all important decisions and decisionmakers. The research focus in this book is obviously limited to trial court activity. Since inequities have often been observed both before and after actual court proceedings, we will be unable to speak to the ultimate question of justice as it applies to the entire criminal justice process in Metro City.[18] We will, however, confront this issue at one of the judicial system's most important stages.

Another question to which no definitive answer is found concerns the meaning of justice in criminal case dispositions. The trend toward individualized treatment and diverse notions about what sanctions are intended to achieve (punishment, retribution, deterrence, incapacitation, rehabilitation) make this determination extremely difficult. An acceptable working definition equates justice with equal treatment of persons in similar legal circumstances.[19] Treatment, either uniform or tailored to the individual defendant, should relate only to legally relevant case or defendant characteristics, making it safe to conclude that significant race-related relationships would, in nearly every situation, be unjust per se.

The absence of information on the prior criminal record of each defendant also poses difficulties. Problems could arise because elsewhere prior record has been linked to both defendant race and sentencing patterns (see chapter 5). For several reasons, however, its omission does not seriously undermine the integrity of this project. In addition to sentencing, decisions where prior record should have no effect (convictions) are also being examined. Being sensitive to the absence of this variable means we will be able at least to estimate the parameters of its possible effects. Also, several trial court inquiries have been able to proceed effectively without data on prior record while others have found record unrelated to race or, occasionally, sentence length.[20] There is no doubt that prior record would be of value here, but we are able to proceed cautiously without it.

Inevitably, data-based court analyses have weaknesses; most also have offsetting strengths. On balance, the positive aspects of the research location and criminal case histories in this study outweigh its shortcomings. Detailed judge and defendant information has been collected over an extended period and encompasses a wide range of criminal activity. Large samples and adequate controls for many legal and extralegal factors minimize the likelihood that the findings will be unrepresentative at the individual case level. These accurately coded autobiographical and behavioral data permit a comprehensive exploration of a black bench and an extensive investigation of black defendant treatment in this major trial court.

Notes

1. General sources have not been listed in order to protect anonymity. Please contact the author directly for more detailed information on the city and court.

2. U.S. Bureau of the Census, *Statistical Abstract of the United States: 1973* (Washington: Government Printing Office, 1973), p. 148.

3. The jurisdiction of the arraignment court was increased from two to five years in July 1971. The chief court administrator believes this change would not have affected the disposition of any cases included here although it kept some cases from reaching the trial court, a selectivity that does not systematically bias the resulting samples. No other major procedural or statutory changes took place during the 1968-1974 period that would have altered the case histories available for analysis.

4. Because they served the same purpose as preliminary hearings, were much more costly, and yet provided little additional defendant protection (95 percent of the defendants not dismissed at preliminary hearings were subsequently indicted), indicting grand juries were abolished after the data reported here were gathered.

5. The exceptions are when the original trial judge became ill or when an out-of-town judge presided at the trial but left the city prior to sentencing. Both types of cases have been omitted from this analysis.

6. Metro City magazine, April 1973.
7. Metro City newspaper, December 28, 1972.
8. Metro City newspaper, July 6, 1973.
9. Personal interview, July 1978.
10. Thomas M. Uhlman and N. Darlene Walker, "Pleas No Bargains?: The Impact of Case Disposition on Sentencing," *Social Science Quarterly* (1979).
11. Thomas M. Uhlman, N. Darlene Walker, and Richard J. Richardson, " 'He Takes Some of My Time: I Take Some of His': An Analysis of Sentencing in Jury Cases," Paper presented at the 1978 annual meeting of the Southwest Social Science Association, Houston, Texas.
12. Roy B. Flemming, Carol W. Kohfeld, and Thomas M. Uhlman, "The Limitations of Bail Reform: A Quasi-Experimental Analysis," Paper presented at the 1979 annual meeting of the American Political Science Association, Washington, D.C.
13. Peter Greenwood et al., *Prosecution of Adult Felony Defendants in Los Angeles County: A Policy Perspective* (Santa Monica, Calif.: The Rand Corporation, 1973); Walter Gray Markham, "Chromatic Justice: Color as an Element of the Offense," Paper presented at the 1974 annual meeting of the American Political Science Association, Chicago.
14. For comparisons to similar sentencing projects, see James Eisenstein and Herbert Jacob, *Felony Justice* (Boston: Little, Brown and Company, 1977); James L. Gibson, "Race as a Determinant of Criminal Sentences: A Methodological Critique and a Case Study," *Law and Society Review* 12 (Spring 1978):455-478; John Hagan, "Extra-Legal Attributes and Criminal Sentencing: An Assessment of a Sociological Viewpoint," *Law and Society Review* 8 (Spring 1974):357-383; Terence P. Thornberry, "Race, Socioeconomic Status and Sentencing in the Juvenile Justice System," *Journal of Criminal Law and Criminology* 64 (1973):90-98.
15. These criteria have been used previously. See Edward Green, *Judicial Attitudes in Sentencing* (New York: St. Martin's Press, 1961), p. 26; George William Baab and William Royal Furgeson, "Texas Sentencing Practices: A Statistical Study," *Texas Law Review* 45 (February 1967):490-491; Charles Engle, "Criminal Justice in the City: A Study of Sentence Severity and Variation in the Philadelphia Criminal Court System," Ph.D. dissertation, Temple University, 1971, pp. 79-80.
16. The rank-ordering of the various types of sentences in this scale is similar to those developed previously by the Administrative Office of the U.S. Courts and other researchers. For the development, discussion, and application of sentencing scales, see Administrative Office of the U.S. Courts, *Federal Offenders in the U.S. District Courts, 1970* (Washington: Government Printing Office, 1972); Beverly Blair Cook, "Sentencing Behavior of Federal Judges: Draft Cases 1972," *University of Cincinnati Law Review* 42 (1973):597-633; James Eisenstein and Herbert Jacob, "Measuring Performance and Outputs of Urban Criminal Courts," *Social Science Quarterly* 54 (March 1974):713-724; Baab and Furgeson, "Texas Sentencing Practices."

17. Hubert M. Blalock, Jr., *Causal Inferences in Nonexperimental Research* (Chapel Hill: University of North Carolina Press, 1964), pp. 34-35; W. Phillips Shively, *The Craft of Political Research* (Englewood Cliffs, N.J.: Prentice-Hall, Inc. 1974), pp. 71-76.

18. U.S. Commission on Civil Rights, *Justice* (Washington: Government Printing Office, 1965); Walter C. Reckless, *The Crime Problem* (New York: Appleton-Century-Crofts, Inc., 1950); David M. Petersen and Paul C. Friday, "Early Release from Incarceration: Race as a Factor in the Use of 'Shock Probation,' " *Journal of Criminal Law and Criminology* 66 (March 1975):79-87.

19. Ernst W. Puttkammer, *Administration of Criminal Law* (Chicago: University of Chicago Press, 1950), p. xviii; Julian D'Esposito, "Sentencing Disparity: Causes and Cures," *Journal of Criminal Law, Criminology, and Police Science* 60 (June 1969):182.

20. Southern Regional Council, *Race Makes the Difference: An Analysis of Sentence Disparity among Black and White Offenders in Southern Prisons* (Atlanta: Southern Regional Council, 1969); Henry Allen Bullock, "Significance of the Racial Factor in the Length of Prison Sentences," *Journal of Criminal Law Criminology and Police Science* 52 (November/December 1961):411-417; Herbert Jacob and James Eisenstein, "Sentences and Other Sanctions in the Criminal Courts of Baltimore, Chicago, and Detroit," *Political Science Quarterly* 90 (Winter 1975/76):617-635.

3 Exceptional Achievements: The Background Characteristics of the Black Bench

As a result of a variety of historical forces, individual handicaps, and exclusionary practices, blacks in the United States have been, and still are, underrepresented in the legal profession. As we have seen, this underrepresentation, although notable elsewhere, is most severe at the capstone of the profession—the judiciary. Notwithstanding recent advances, the black bench remains a small but important and little understood political elite.[1]

While black judicial success is an exceptional achievement, judgeships are generally reserved for exceptionally qualified individuals. It has yet to be determined whether "exceptional" background characteristics and career patterns differ by judicial race. By utilizing detailed autobiographical statements, this issue is investigated for the sixteen black and seventy-nine white jurists serving on the Metro City trial bench. Points of comparison include local and regional ties of the judges, their educations, prejudicial careers, methods of selection, and professional and community involvement.

In addition to placing black judicial careers in perspective, interracial comparisons provide at least partial answers to questions concerning minority group elite recruitment and representation. Contrasting personal attributes by judicial race may uncover both race-related criteria conducive to judicial selection and biases present in the recruitment process. In this regard, particular attention is given to informal or unofficial prerequisites for judicial service. Equally important, these comparisons gauge the diversity on the court and by implication the "representativeness" of the black bench.

Background studies are certainly not new to judicial research, with descriptive projects being the most common. These are usually efforts to gather and interpret as many relevant facts as possible about the characteristics of past, present, or future jurists.[2] Background research may do more than describe the types of individuals who assume judicial positions. Exercising caution, scholars have also attempted to establish a link between judges' backgrounds and subsequent behavior. Doubts remain over how firm the relationship is, but in some courts the decisional and policy-making activities of judges are apparently related to certain aspects of their social backgrounds and political experiences. If they are not, it is argued that knowing judges' personal characteristics still enables us to better evaluate the jobs they are doing.[3] Even this more modest goal suffices here. Given our limited knowledge and the significance of race as a background characteristic, it becomes almost mandatory to explore as many aspects of the black judicial experience as possible, ignoring for the moment the possibility of a behavioral linkage. We can begin by describing the black bar in Metro City, the source of black judicial recruits.

The Black Bar in Metro City

With few exceptions, the black legal experience in Metro City parallels the general patterns described in chapter one. Historically, few blacks have become legal professionals. The first black lawyer appeared in the city following the Civil War. By 1900 only five had viable practices and another five were struggling to exist as attorneys. Between 1900 and 1945 fewer than thirty blacks were admitted to the bar. About 100 gained entry during the next twenty-five years, and today only about 300 are practicing in a city with 6,700 attorneys. No more than twenty blacks have presided on either the arraignment or trial benches at any time. Overall, Metro City ranks tenth best out of twenty-four Northern cities in its ratio of black judges to black population.

In Metro City, limited legal opportunities have resulted from apparent biases in law school admissions and the administration of the state bar examination. As recently as 1966, there were probably no more than a dozen black law students in six predominantly white law schools in the state. Black enrollment increased substantially during the past decade and then apparently reached a plateau. Today, approximately 8 percent of the law graduates are black.

A blue-ribbon bar association committee established in 1970 to investigate charges of bias in the administration of the bar examination discovered that during the preceding fifteen years guarantees of candidate anonymity could have been breached. Not only were the law examiners able to match test papers to applicants, but they also had access to personal data on individuals, including photographs. In addition, the examiners had the discretion to upgrade and eventually pass marginal papers. Perhaps as a consequence of candidate identification and examiner discretion, the committee reported that graduates from the fully accredited but predominantly black Howard University Law School were much less likely to pass the bar than non-Howard black graduates (15.5 percent Howard versus 33.5 percent non-Howard). More striking, Howard graduates were even less likely to pass the examination than white candidates *without* a law degree, 22.7 percent of whom passed.

The bar examination story recounted by one black judge is quite revealing:

> I failed the first time I took the bar examination. I was two months out of law school; I had studied; I was single with no other concerns. It should have been the best opportunity for me to pass. After being released from the Army two years later, I passed the bar without studying nearly as hard. At that time I had a wife, lived in a cramped

three bedroom apartment with children; I was working and my mother-in-law was there. I don't know for certain whether there was discrimination the first time, but it always has seemed so to me.

The careers of black practitioners in Metro City have been, and for many continue to be, difficult. In the past, the attitude of most white judges toward black attorneys was one of sufferance. Others were more openly hostile. One black judge remembers that as a young attorney he arrived at court early one morning, waited all day while cases brought by white lawyers were being heard, and finally was asked by the presiding judge in a nearly empty courtroom, "Boy, do you have any business here?" Another painfully recalls overhearing one judge talk to another about him: "How can you expect any better? They're just out of the jungle."

Blatant discrimination like this is rare today, but other problems remain. Most black attorneys in private practice deal extensively with criminal and domestic matters. A black judge recently elected to the bench said, "My practice was about 70 percent criminal. I had to scramble all the time; I often retained new clients while at arraignment court hearings for old ones. If you had style and flair, you could get clients who had been arrested and were at the courthouse without lawyers." Unfortunately, many of these clients are also poor; nearly all are black. Fees are usually small, and collection becomes difficult, if not impossible, at times. "We had no problems getting clients," an older black attorney observed, "But there was a resource problem. Both the businesses and individuals couldn't afford retainers, so we had to make up for this in volume."

Black employment opportunities in the city's predominantly white firms have expanded recently, but many small and moderate-sized firms have not yet integrated while some larger ones have seen fit only to hire at token levels. As a group, black lawyers in the city view themselves as having inferior career opportunities, lower pay, and lesser status than their white counterparts.

A significant question to ask in light of this assessment is whether the black bench is "randomly" selected from the pool of available black legal talent in the city. If the answer is no, then is the black recruitment pattern more comparable to the pattern in evidence for the white judiciary? Understanding judicial localism in Metro City is helpful in addressing these issues.

Localism—Birthplace, Childhood, Education

Investigations of both state and federal benches indicate that close community and regional ties are important informal or unofficial prerequisites for judicial service.[4] By allowing one to develop career contacts, be visible professionally, and establish a reputation for honesty and integrity, localism becomes a highly valued asset in the process of judicial selection. Four widely employed measures determine whether black and white Metro City judges differ in the local associations they either maintained or developed during their formative years. They are: where the judges were born and raised and where they attended college and law school.

Although early local ties are a hallmark of the entire Metro City bench, racial differences do emerge. An extremely high proportion of the white bench is native to the area. Fifty-seven future white jurists (86.8 percent) were born in the city or state, and sixty-three (94.7 percent) were raised there. By comparison, the black bench is significantly more diverse geographically. Seven of the sixteen blacks (43.8 percent) were born and five (31.3 percent) were raised out of state.[5]

Because Metro City is fortunate in having several outstanding institutions of higher learning, many future jurists stayed near home to acquire both their undergraduate and legal educations. But again significant racial differences exist. White college and law school attendance is 69.3 percent and 85.9 percent, respectively, while similar figures for blacks are only 25.0 and 62.5 percent. The pattern is essentially reversed for out-of-state college and law school enrollment (white: 16.0 percent college, 6.4 percent law school; black: 50.0 percent college, 37.5 percent law school).[6]

The distribution of "extreme" cases provides a final perspective on localism within the judiciary. In a study of state supreme court judges, Bradley Canon calculates how many individuals are "complete locals."[7] By adopting a similar approach, a majority of the white judges (57.9 percent) are classified as Metro City locals—born, raised, and educated in the *city*. Only two blacks (12.5 percent) have that distinction. Conversely, only one white jurist out of a group of seventy-nine (1.3 percent) is a complete nonlocal (born, raised, and educated outside the *state*) compared to four blacks (25 percent). Thus, being a complete nonlocal and then becoming a judge is nearly impossible for a white person but a reasonable expectation for otherwise qualified blacks.

Although localism remains a hallmark of the Metro City judiciary, interracial differences exist. The pattern is consistent from birth to law school as black judges more frequently than white were born, raised, and educated outside Metro City and state. Recent changes in the racial and ethnic makeup of urban population centers may explain part of the disparity. Black out-migration from the South and in-migration to Northern metropolitan regions, while having slowed in recent years, characterized the preceding quarter century. Metro City was no exception to this trend, and judicial origins reflect this broad, race-related shift in population patterns. Of the seven nonlocal black jurists, five were born and raised in the South.[8]

Also, limited black educational opportunities within the city and state may have compelled many of these future jurists to seek schooling elsewhere. No predominantly black colleges are located in the city, and no black law schools

Background Characteristics of the Black Bench   49

are located in either the city or the state. Thus, attendance by blacks at educational institutions outside the area would have been necessary were restrictive and/or discriminatory admissions practices in effect at local institutions. Precise information on the extent and duration of these practices is not readily available. But minimal black enrollment figures challenge the notion that a legal education was available locally to all qualified black applicants.

Finally, the pool of eligible black judicial candidates is restricted by the still limited number of black attorneys. With other criteria perhaps more important in selection, the informal localism prerequisite may be more easily waived for qualified black candidates.

Education—College and Law School Attendance

An informal requirement for judicial office that is not waived is a quality education. Available data indicate that the entire Metro City bench is exceptionally well educated with only marginal interracial differences. Ordinarily the absence of a significant relationship fails to generate much interest. But such a finding is noteworthy because it reveals distinguishing characteristics of the black Americans who successfully attain coveted seats on the Metro City bench.

In outlining the educational credentials of the judiciary, a useful starting point is a description of the types of colleges and law schools future jurists attended. Following the lead of Sheldon Goldman, educational institutions are classified as Ivy League, non-Ivy public, and non-Ivy private.[9] Tables 3-1 and 3-2 present these groupings broken down by judicial race.

The lack of significance in the summary statistics indicates the absence of broad differences between black and white judges within this general typology of educational institutions. Both groups attended non-Ivy League public colleges and non-Ivy private law schools in nearly equal proportions. The most notable

Table 3-1
Type of College Attended by Judicial Race
(percent)

	Ivy League	Non-Ivy Public	Non-Ivy Private	None
Black judges	6.3	31.3	62.5	0
(N = 16)	(1)	(5)	(10)	(0)
White judges	25.3	29.3	38.7	6.7
(N = 75)	(19)	(22)	(29)	(5)
Total	22.0	29.7	42.9	5.5
(N = 91)	(20)	(27)	(39)	(5)

Chi square = 5.02; sig. = not significant.

Table 3-2
Type of Law School Attended by Judicial Race
(percent)

	Ivy League	Non-Ivy Public	Non-Ivy Private
Black judges	31.3	50.0	18.8
(N = 16)	(5)	(8)	(3)
White judges	47.4	37.2	15.4
(N = 78)	(37)	(29)	(12)
Total	44.7	39.4	16.0
(N = 94)	(42)	(37)	(15)

Chi square = 1.43; sig. = not significant.

differences are the higher rate of Ivy League attendance for whites and, at the other end of the spectrum, the lack of a college education for five white judges.[10]

The prestige attached to an Ivy League education for the whites is largely offset by impressive black scholarly achievements in other areas. A greater percentage of the black bench than the white graduated Phi Beta Kappa, received other college or law school honors, and engaged in nonlegal graduate work.[11]

The educational accomplishments of the Metro City judiciary carry a special meaning for its black members. Although black and white academic achievements are comparable, the minority group justices have overcome prohibitive odds against any black receiving the quality education they received at the time they received it. Only in the mid-to-late 1960s did legal training at predominantly white institutions become a realistic possibility for black Americans. Exclusionary practices were also evident in Metro City and state law schools. Because of this admissions barrier, blacks entering white institutions in the preenlightened era prior to the mid-1960s needed exceptional credentials to qualify as representatives of their race.

In this context it becomes important to note that a majority of the black bench in Metro City attended law school during this dark age in race relations and also graduated from predominantly white, Ivy League, or state institutions (table 3-3). In fact, most had completed their legal studies before the mid-1950s, a time when many public schools remained segregated and a college education, let alone a legal education, was an unattainable dream for nearly every black child.

John Schmidhauser states that a good education is perhaps of greatest importance in the formative period of future judges' career patterns and development.[12] Considered in this light, the Metro City judiciary as a whole and its black component in particular are indeed fortunate. However, the informal requirement of educational excellence, especially excellence achieved at an Ivy

**Table 3-3
Black Metro City Judges—Years Admitted to Law School and
Type of Law School Attended**

Years Admitted to Law School	Percentage	N
1920-1929	6.3	1
1930-1939	6.3	1
1940-1949	50.0	8
1950-1959	12.5	2
1960-1964	12.5	2
1965-present	0	0
Missing	12.5	2

Type of Law School	Percentage	N
Ivy League	31.3	5
Metro state	43.8	7
Other state	6.3	1
Predominantly black	18.8	3

League or state law school, also functions as a major and perhaps unnecessary barrier to judicial opportunities. While many judicial aspirants suffer as a result, collectively minority group members are hurt the most. Recent history indicates that exclusionary practices coupled with inadequate preparation have sharply restricted black educational opportunities. The Metro City experience indicates that the requisite prejudicial educational credentials have been denied to all but a few remarkably successful blacks.[13]

**Prejudicial Careers—Prosecutorial Experience,
Government Employment, Private Practice**

Since Joseph Schlesinger's seminal work on political ambition, the career and employment histories of various elite groups have generated considerable research interest.[14] In addition to producing a greater understanding of common attitudes and socializing experiences, these investigations occasionally uncover consistent patterns of opportunity where one position contributes to subsequent advancement and success. Although less frequent and often less sophisticated, similar explorations have yielded valuable insights into the practice and process of judicial recruitment.[15]

One of these insights is the relative frequency with which future jurists share prior prosecutorial experience.[16] This relationship also holds in Metro City, as nearly two-thirds of the judges (63.8 percent) engaged in prosecutorial work. While percentage differences exist, this activity was important in the prejudicial careers of both black (87.5 percent, N = 14) and white (59.0 percent, N = 46) (difference not significant) jurists. Notably, however, the path between the prosecutor's office and the judge's chambers was by no means direct.

A prosecutorial position functioned primarily as a "base office" or career entry point for future Metro City jurists.[17] Fewer than 8 percent of them were elevated to the bench directly from prosecutorial positions. This figure represents a sharp drop from the 64 percent who report experience in this office. Again the pattern applies across judicial race; early prosecutorial work was usually abandoned by both blacks and whites in favor of other prejudicial employment.

These other career options appear in table 3-4. Bypassing political positions to be dealt with separately, three additional "penultimate offices" or positions held immediately prior to a seat on the Metro City trial bench are listed. Previous experience is in evidence for only one judge. Formerly a lower court magistrate, he had been elevated to the trial bench years ago. Government experience, excluding political and prosecutorial activity, also appears infrequently. Rather than being absent, like prosecutorial work, it emerges as a relatively early stop in a prejudicial career.

Substantial minorities of both black (43.8 percent) and white (28.6 percent) (difference not significant) judges have been local, state, or federal employees. The jobs themselves differ substantially, but they have a common bond in that nearly all require legal expertise.[18] Therefore, government and prosecutorial work both served as important "base offices" and usually came before private practice—the most common penultimate office in a prejudicial career.

Engaging in private practice either independently or as an associate or partner in a firm is another characteristic that a majority of the Metro City judiciary (75.6 percent) shares. This activity just prior to judicial service appears with nearly equal frequency in the careers of black (66.7 percent) and white (77.6 percent) judges. Interracial conformity is further highlighted by observing the type of practice that the future jurists pursued.

Table 3-4
Prejudicial Career Positions by Judicial Race
(percent)

	Prosecutorial	Governmental	Private Practice	Political	Judicial
Black judges	13.3	20.0	66.7	0	0
(N = 15)	(2)	(3)	(10)	(0)	(0)
White judges	5.9	9.1	77.6	5.9	1.5
(N = 67)	(4)	(6)	(52)	(4)	(1)
Total	7.3	11.0	75.6	4.9	1.2
(N = 82)	(6)	(9)	(62)	(4)	(1)

Chi square = 3.60; sig. = not significant.

Sheldon Goldman distinguishes between small and large law firms and ascribes socioeconomic characteristics to both.[19] The functional equivalent for blacks in the legal profession may be private practice or association with a firm. Most black attorneys remain individual practitioners; a majority of the black judges responding to one survey report never having joined a private firm.[20] The pattern within the black bar in Metro City is similar; most black attorneys in private practice have been and continue to be sole practitioners. While they frequently participate in overhead sharing arrangements or informal associations, formal partnerships are not common. Even more unusual are predominantly black firms. Four or five relatively small firms (averaging about five members) exist today with all but one being of recent vintage.

In contrast, the private practices among black jurists were markedly different. Association with a firm at some stage in their careers was common as about half (eight of fifteen, or 53.3 percent) indicate such affiliations. Not surprisingly, nearly all were associated with the one well-established black firm that was in existence throughout the period. However, several others departed from common practice even further by being employed by predominantly white firms in the city. Almost two-thirds of the whites in private practice (62.0 percent) also affiliated with law firms prior to their judicial careers. In this respect then, black jurists are clearly more comparable to their white judicial colleagues than to a cross section of the city's black bar.

The results of a similar background investigation prompted Henry Glick and Kenneth Vines to conclude that, "There is ... no career route that is standard preparation for judges, and they have held a variety of posts...."[21] While judges in Metro City also held a variety of posts, these positions form a distinguishable pattern in prejudicial employment. The significance of the pattern is enhanced in that it applies to both black and white judicial candidates.

All judges actively pursue their legal careers in one form or another. The specifics vary, but "hands on" legal work emerges as another unofficial prerequisite for office. Government service as a prosecutor or in another legal capacity early in the future judge's career is the norm and functions as a solid career base. Private practice, an intermediate career step usually consisting of membership in a law firm, represents both a mark of success and an association helpful to judicial prospects. Success here in conjunction with prior government service constitutes the baseline around which both black and white judicial candidacies in Metro City can be and have been structured.

Prejudicial Careers—Political Involvement

Prejudicial careers may also vary in degree of partisan political activity. Political involvement is treated separately because of the major role that political considerations have played in the selection of most jurists.[22] Political ideology or quasi-ideology is usually an important factor in selection, with party identification frequently used as an easy, though often inaccurate, reference in gauging an individual's views. Identification with a major political party during a judge's career is required in Metro City; judicial candidates either initially run on a partisan ballot or are appointed by the governor to fill an unexpired term and then must face reelection under a party standard.

Seventy-five percent (twelve) of the blacks and 55 percent of the whites (forty-three) are affiliated with the Democratic party. The interracial difference of 20 percent is again not large enough to signify interdependence between the variables. That a majority of judges of both races are Democrats is not particularly surprising in light of the city's strongly Democratic electorate in recent years. More noteworthy is the substantial Republican presence among the black judiciary (25 percent). This rather high representation, at least when contrasted to the extremely strong electoral bond between minority group members and the Democratic party, possibly describes membership in the black upper class and clearly demonstrates the governor's ability to control appointments to a limited number of judicial positions in the city.[23] Three of the four black Republicans were initially appointed by a Republican governor over standard opposition by the Democratic organization. By their continued presence on the bench, several of these black Republicans also display their instincts for political survival. After having been appointed, they sought and received the backing of both political parties in their bids for election to full ten-year terms on the bench.

Party identification becomes more important when linked to prior political activity. In other words, political considerations during a prejudicial career may be hypothesized as being of greater significance if there is also evidence of active partisan involvement. In Metro City a majority of both the black (75.0 percent) and white (58.4 percent) jurists report no prejudicial political activity. Most of those who did participate undertook yeoman tasks and avoided high-visibility positions.[24] The lack of emphasis on partisan activity is also indicated by the infrequent emergence of judges from the political ranks. As seen in table 3-4, only four judges (4.9 percent) were holding political positions immediately prior to selection.[25]

This does not mean that judges are elevated to the bench without political scrutiny. Their qualifications for judicial service and their political credentials are both carefully checked by party officials. In fact, interviews revealed that while visible partisanship might not be required or at least not reported, many future jurists had supported their party behind the scenes; and these credits were indeed helpful for prospective candidates. The comments of one black judge are typical: "I wouldn't consider myself a party regular; I wasn't a party hack. But on the other hand, I wasn't devoid of political connections or activity. My ward leader knew me and put forward my name."

While partisan loyalty seems to be important, extensive and, in particular, highly visible political activity does not represent an informal requirement for a successful judicial candidacy in Metro City. Important in understanding the entire recruitment process, this finding is especially significant for the black bench when compared to the rather high levels of political activity observed on the part of black attorneys. Political involvement is viewed as an avenue for advancement in black communities, and a majority of black attorneys see it as such.[26] Thus the limited nature of this activity by black jurists may be viewed as a special characteristic of the bench.[27] It differentiates these individuals from the majority of black legal professionals and perhaps makes them more acceptable to the white legal establishment.

Professional and Community Activities

Henderson and Sinclair report that bar association activity is a "must" for judicial office seekers in Texas.[28] It is also a must in Metro City. Over 90 percent of both the black and white benches are city and county bar association members while over 80 percent of both judicial groups also belong to the state bar.[29] American Bar Association membership is less common, but notably it is less common for both because only about 50 percent of the black and white benches have joined. A significant interracial difference occurs as expected, in membership in the National Bar Association. Half of the black judges in Metro City are members of this relatively new black legal organization.

Professional activity is more than bar association membership. Taking the Henderson and Sinclair approach one step further, the number of professional affiliations of any type reported by each judge is also tabulated. This list includes law school alumni organizations, lawyers' clubs, bench-bar conference committees, and conferences of trial lawyers and judges. Wide-ranging professional involvement is common for most Metro City judges. Two-thirds of the court indicate more than four such memberships, and one-third indicate seven or more. No significant interracial differences exist; broad-based professional activity plays an important role in the careers of nearly all Metro City jurists.

Like political activity, extensive community involvement contributes to black success within the legal profession in Metro City and elsewhere.[30] In this case, however, the behavior of the black bench and bar are similar. All black Metro City jurists are active in community functions that include public service, public affairs, and religious and social organizations. The high degree of their extrajudicial involvement is evidenced by the ten judges participating in more than ten activities and associations. Surprisingly, this extensive activity often fails to include membership in civil rights organizations. Only eight black judges (50 percent) list any civil rights associations in their autobiographical statements. One judge who was active in the civil rights struggle observed, "As a group, we have not been real activists. At times we've had to be pushed."

Thus extensive community involvement is centrally located in the lives and probably the careers of black jurists. Their interests are wide-ranging and include many activities far removed from the "traditional" ones of law and civil rights.

By comparison, white Metro City judges are not quite as involved in the community as are their black colleagues. Although a significant interracial difference exists (significance = .05), whites cannot be categorized as inactive. Nearly two-thirds (63.5 percent) are members of at least six different organizations. This race-related disparity, while larger than others, is still one of degree with white judges active in community affairs and blacks extremely active. Regardless of race, the vast majority of Metro City jurists are highly visible members of their profession as well as their community.

Method of Judicial Selection

Methods of judicial selection are critical to the hopes and aspirations of those favoring increased minority group judicial representation. The procedures involved, formal and informal, official and unofficial, have determined the past and will shape the future of the black bench. This topic embraces a variety of issues. Some have already been touched on in analyzing judicial background characteristics. Others dealt with here concern the relationships between different formal selection methods and black judicial success.

As described in chapter 2, a seat on the Metro City bench initially is attained by one of two clearly separable routes—appointment or election. All judges must run for reelection on a partisan ballot and later on a retention basis. Their critical entry to the bench, however, is gained either through gubernatorial appointment or by partisan election victories in a primary (if necessary) and then a general election. These two approaches have generated considerable debate concerning their relative advantages for increased black judicial representation.[31]

Although the debate itself cannot be resolved here, methods of black judicial selection in Metro City add data to it that are both clear and one-sided. Of the sixteen black jurists in the sample, fifteen (93.8 percent) were initially *appointed* while only one (6.2 percent) was first elected.

In theory, the elective approach appears well suited to advancing black judicial interests, particularly in urban areas where blacks have acquired substantial electoral power. These data indicate, however, that Metro City blacks, over one-fourth of the city's electorate, have been unable to take advantage of their power at the ballot box to create a viable route to the bench. Considering the past and present strength of the party organizations and the absence of an effective black political coalition, this failure is not surprising. Instead, black political elites are required to work within the party organizations to promote black judicial candidates. This situation means that in the end success still depends to a considerable degree on "enlightened" white political leadership.

The obvious follow-up issue is to determine how dependent white judicial candidates are on the blessings of the same political leaders. They too rely, although not as overwhelmingly, on judicial appointments for initial access to the bench. Sixty-eight percent (fifty-four) were first appointed, an insignificant difference from black selection. However, party leaders also exercise tight control over those who succeed via election. Interview and autobiographical data indicate that every successful judicial candidate, when he or she first ran, had party endorsements in both the primary and general elections; a white or black judicial insurgent has yet to be elected in Metro City.

Evidence that judges in the city are cleared by the political leadership appears to have a direct bearing on the relationships or, perhaps more appropriately, the nonrelationships examined. Regardless of racial identification, most judicial background characteristics and prejudicial careers in Metro City are similar. Discounting the possibilities of chance occurrence, one looks for a unifying mechanism or influence. That influence seems to be provided by the formal and informal procedures involved in judicial selection.

This is not a novel idea. Herbert Jacob concludes that "... formal selection procedures are more than a facade ... they are likely to affect the nominating process by establishing certain informal qualifications, by giving access to particular categorical groups, or by placing some individuals at an advantage ... for particular offices."[32] Such an assessment is supported by the Metro City example—an example that underlines the control exercised by the political leadership. Apparently in Metro City the informal and formal requirements are joined, and what emerges is a strikingly similar collection of jurists.

Conclusions

Race-related background differences are minimal on the Metro City bench. Disparities appear, but they occur less frequently and are usually smaller than hypothesized. This finding has implications regarding both the pattern of judicial recruitment in the city and the current state of the black bench.

Emerging as important in the eventual composition of the Metro City judiciary is a series of informal requirements or prerequisites for judicial service. Characteristics such as localism, a quality education, prosecutorial experience, private practice, limited political involvement, and extensive professional and community activities, while not legally mandated, are experiences and qualifications that a large majority of the trial court judges share. They apparently become important elements in a candidacy by making an individual desirable to party leaders and the electorate as well as by placing him in positions for self-advancement. The unifying mechanism in the recruitment process is the control exercised by the political elite. By determining which candidates will succeed, the political leadership effectively defines what these informal requirements will be.

This finding leads directly to others regarding the blacks who have become judges in Metro City. Jerome Shuman concludes that black lawyers in his study are "... Black first and lawyers second."[33] A comparable statement is more difficult to support for the blacks now serving on the Metro City bench. Blackness is an obvious and important factor in their backgrounds, but it is not the only factor. The close correspondence between black and white judicial career patterns and credentials appears to be equally significant.

Black judges in Metro City have met and at times surpassed the informal standards applied to their white colleagues. Members of an educated elite, they have touched the right bases in terms of the legal profession, government service, and community involvement. They have secured their positions as members of the "establishment." Only upon reaching this level of achievement are blacks successful as candidates for judicial office. Certainly the career and educational accomplishments of the white jurists are also impressive. But in relative terms black judges' achievements appear greater because they had further to go and had a greater number of obstacles placed in their paths. The "required" educational and career credentials are, by any measure, harder for blacks to acquire than whites.

Many judicial scholars believe that judgeships should be restricted to those who, regardless of race, have compiled exceptional education and career successes.[34] However, the important issue, especially as it pertains to black representation, is whether several of the informal prerequisites uncovered (state or Ivy League law school attendance, prosecutorial work, law firm ties, limited political experience) contribute materially to quality judicial performance or merely indicate membership in the higher echelons of the legal establishment— both of which are by no means synonymous or even necessarily related.

Restricting black judgeships to the select few who fit the dominant white recruitment pattern challenges, in part at least, the principles of group representation. While attributes are not perfectly linked to the more accurate measures of representation such as attitudes and decisions, a positive relationship is presumed to exist—hence the concept of descriptive representation.[35] Analyzed by the criteria available, the black bench in Metro City is not descriptively representative of the black community. More importantly, nor is it descriptively representative of the entire black legal community. Most black attorneys in the city have not gone to Ivy League schools, have not engaged in prosecutorial work, and have not avoided active political involvement.

Extremely "safe" blacks appear to have been the primary recruits to the Metro City bench while a broader cross section of the black bar has been underrepresented. Quality black law school graduates, public defenders, community lawyers, and individual practitioners may also have much to offer a court. To date they have not really been given the opportunity as the black bench in Metro City remains an extraordinary subset of the black legal fraternity.

Notes

1. To date, empirical research on the black judiciary has been limited to three analyses of the black bench. See Beverly Blair Cook, "Black Representation in the Third Branch," *Black Law Journal* 1 (Winter 1971):260-279; "The Black Judge in America," *Judicature* 57 (June/July 1973):18-25. Black judicial responses were also tabulated separately in Jerome Shuman, "A Black Lawyers Study," *Howard Law Journal* 16 (Winter 1971):225-313. The primary strength of the Shuman and *Judicature* surveys is their scope; both include a large percentage of the black judicial population. With this strength, however, comes the problem that there really is no "national" black bench, and in trying to study black judges everywhere, distinguishing characteristics in each jurisdiction that influence recruitment, selection, and behavior are lost. A second difficulty is that these projects do not make comparisons to other judicial groups and therefore fail to provide another perspective that would add meaning to the black judge data.

2. For example, see John R. Schmidhauser, "The Justices of the Supreme Court: A Collective Portrait," *Midwest Journal of Political Science* 3 (February 1959):1-57; Herbert Jacob, "The Effect of Institutional Differences in the Recruitment Process: The Case of State Judges," *Journal of Public Law* 13 (1964):104-119; Sheldon Goldman, "Characteristics of Eisenhower and Kennedy Appointees to the Lower Federal Court," *Western Political Quarterly* 18 (December 1965):755-762; Richard J. Richardson and Kenneth Vines, *The Politics of the Federal Courts* (Boston: Little, Brown and Company, 1970), pp. 56-79; Bradley Canon, "Characteristics and Career Patterns of State Supreme Court Justices," *State Government* 65 (Winter 1972):34-41.

3. Bradley C. Canon, "The Impact of Formal Selection Processes on the Characteristics of Judges—Reconsidered," *Law and Society Review* 6 (May 1972): 579; Henry Robert Glick and Kenneth Vines, *State Court Systems* (Englewood Cliffs, N.J.: Prentice-Hall, Inc., 1973), p. 47; Joel Grossman, "Social Backgrounds and Judicial Decision-Making," *Harvard Law Review* 79 (June 1966):1562.

4. Glick and Vines, *State Court Systems,* pp. 57-58; Canon, "Characteristics and Career Patterns," p. 37; Kenneth Vines, "Federal District Judges and Race Relations Cases in the South," *Journal of Politics* 26 (1964):337-357.

5. The differences between judicial race and these localism characteristics are both statistically significant (significance = .05). Localism is trichotomized. Categories are born or raised in Metro City; Metro state; or out of state. Cramer's V, the appropriate measure of association, equals .32 relating judicial race to birthplace and .35 in the relationship between race and childhood upbringing.

6. These interracial differences are also statistically significant (.05). Cramer's V is .42 relating college location (Metro City, Metro state, outside Metro state) to judicial race and .37 relating race to a similar categorization of law schools.

7. Canon, "Characteristics and Career Patterns," p. 37.

8. The state most frequently represented is South Carolina (three) followed by Louisiana and Oklahoma (one each). Two Northeastern states, Massachusetts and New York, contributed the remaining nonlocal blacks to the bench.

9. Goldman, "Eisenhower and Kennedy Appointees," p. 757.

10. The Metro City bench even fares well on the negative end of an imaginary educational scale. While there are five white judges in the city who do not have undergraduate degrees, every judge has a law degree. As recently as 1969, nearly 8 percent of the state *supreme court* judges in the country had not obtained law degrees; see Glick and Vines, *State Court Systems,* p. 48.

11. Specific percentages for the black ($N = 16$) and the white ($N = 64$) judges are Phi Beta Kappa, 12.5 percent black, 3.1 percent white; other honors, 50 percent black, 37.7 percent white; other graduate work, 25.0 percent black, 4.7 percent white.

12. John R. Schmidhauser, *The Supreme Court: Its Politics, Personalities, and Procedures* (New York: Holt, Rinehart and Winston, 1960), p. 43.

13. The future appears brighter. As the right/opportunity of blacks to attend these established legal institutions increases, so does the pool of eligible judicial candidates. Only time will tell, however, whether this expansion of quality black legal talent will translate into greater minority group judicial representation.

14. Joseph Schlesinger, *Ambition and Politics* (Chicago: Rand McNally & Company, 1966). See also Roger H. Davidson, *The Role of the Congressman* (New York: Pegasus, 1969), chap. 2; John W. Soule, "Future Political Ambitions and the Behavior of Incumbent State Legislators," *Midwest Journal of Political Science* 13 (August 1969):439-454; Leo M. Snowiss, "Congressional Recruitment and Representation," *American Political Science Review* 60 (September 1966):627-639.

15. Some examples are Joel B. Grossman, *Lawyers and Judges: The A.B.A. and the Politics of Judicial Selection* (New York: John Wiley & Sons, Inc., 1965); Harold W. Chase, "Federal Judges: The Appointing Process," *Minnesota Law Review* 51 (1966):185-218; Sheldon Goldman, "Judicial Appointments to the United States Courts of Appeals," *Wisconsin Law Review* (Winter 1967):186-214.

16. Canon, "Characteristics and Career Patterns," pp. 39-40.

17. The terms *base office* and *penultimate office* are borrowed from Schlesinger, *Ambition and Politics,* pp. 70, 90.

18. Examples of this type of work include deputy insurance commissioner; assistant director, Legislative Reference Bureau; counsel, Register of Wills; attorney/examiner, Bureau of Sales and Use Tax; analyst, State Legislative Budget and Finance Committee.

19. Goldman, "Eisenhower and Kennedy Appointees," p. 758.

20. Frederick Brown, "The Black Lawyer in Private Practice," *Harvard Law School Bulletin* 22 (February 1971):13-14; "The Black Judge in America," p. 21.

21. Glick and Vines, *State Court Systems*, p. 49.

22. See Glick and Vines, *State Court Systems*, p. 50; and Goldman, "Judicial Appointments," pp. 186-214.

23. Lucius Barker and Jesse McCorry, *Black Americans and the Political System* (Cambridge, Mass.: Winthrop Publishers, Inc., 1976), p. 106.

24. Examples of this type of activity include counsel for a party committee, membership on a county committee, and convention delegate or alternate.

25. These men, all white, were a congressman, a member of the state house, an insurance commissioner, and a state treasurer. The possibility exists that once on the bench, judges might desire to downplay their partisan political past. If so, their autobiographical statements could underestimate the extent of prior political activity.

26. Brown, "The Black Lawyer," pp. 13-15; and Shuman, "A Black Lawyers Study," p. 299. Focusing on the black bench and bar is not to imply that political considerations are unimportant in the white legal community; they obviously are.

27. The Metro City figures are close to the data on the national black judiciary. See Shuman, "A Black Lawyers Study" and "The Black Judge in America."

28. Bancroft C. Henderson and T.C. Sinclair, *The Selection of Judges in Texas: An Exploratory Study* (Houston, Texas: Public Affairs Center, University of Houston, 1965), p. 63.

29. Because of the manner in which the judges responded to these items, it was difficult at times to distinguish between past, present, and continuing affiliations. Based on the patterns established in reports where dates were listed, the general assumption is made that an extensive listing indicates a high level of activity in the past. In other words, professional and civic visibility are assumed to precede judicial success as well as parallel it.

30. Brown, "The Black Lawyer," p. 14; Shuman, "A Black Lawyers Study," p. 299.

31. For example, see George Crockett, "The Role of the Black Judge," *Journal of Public Law* 29 (1971):391-400; Gilbert Ware, "Introduction to Proceedings: Founding Convention of the Judicial Council of the National Bar Association," *Journal of Public Law* 20 (1971):371-373; "The Black Judge in America," pp. 18-25; Harold M. Baron, "Black Powerlessness in Chicago," *Transaction* 6 (November 1968):27-33.

32. Jacob, "The Effect of Institutional Differences," p. 105. See also Glenn Winters, "The Merit Plan for Judicial Selection and Tenure—Its Historical Development," *Duquesne University Law Review* 7 (Fall 1968):61-78; Canon, "The Impact of Formal Selection Processes," p. 580.

33. Shuman, "A Black Lawyers Study," pp. 228-229.

34. The distinguished black jurist, Raymond Pace Alexander, is included among these scholars. See "The Selection and Education of the Judiciary—Some Unfinished Tasks," *Pennsylvania Bar Association Quarterly* 40 (October 1968):57-67.

35. Paul E. Peterson, "Forms of Representation: Participation of the Poor in Community Action Programs," *American Political Science Review* 64 (June 1970):491-507; Hanna Pitkin, *The Concept of Representation* (Berkeley: University of California Press, 1967).

4
Indistinguishable Performance: The Decision Making of Black Judges

Black elites in the United States have been the subject of a number of inquiries in recent years. As the pace of black advancement quickened in the post-*Brown* era, scholars focused on a variety of black elite groups in attempts to measure, explain, and interpret their newfound success.[1] Within this expanding body of research, one subject has been conspicuously absent. To date, systematic explorations of black decision making have been virtually nonexistent.[2] This chapter focuses on this missing behavioral link by studying the decision-making activity of the black jurists in Metro City.

Black judges fill a special representative role within the legal order. For minority group defendants questioning the fundamental fairness of the criminal justice system, they symbolize hope and encouragement. For members of a black community where powerlessness has confirmed feelings of inferiority, they represent a direct challenge to negative stereotypes. And for some whites, their presence contradicts the all-too-common assumption that the jobs blacks hold are always at or near the bottom of the occupational ladder—a supposition linked to the creation and maintenance of prejudicial attitudes.

The black judicial role is frequently more than symbolic. Stemming from a sensitivity to a variety of inequities observed within their courtrooms, black judges see themselves as educators, reformers, and advocates for social change. Their unique symbolic and substantive role within the legal order may also yield distinctive behavioral patterns. Stuart Nagel hypothesized that it does:

> If the decisional propensities of [black] judges could be compared with those of white judges sitting on the same cases at the trial court level..., one might expect to find that the [black] judges have a higher propensity than the white judges for what might be considered the liberal positions in the cases involved.[3]

A counterargument also appears plausible. The atypically successful black prejudicial careers discussed in chapter 3, a rigorous process of legal socialization, and special scrutiny for highly visible black jurists may attenuate behavioral differences between black and white judges. The issue, however, involves more than accepting or rejecting a null hypothesis.

During the past twenty years, a start has been made toward equalizing political, economic, and social opportunities for people in the United States regardless of race. The moral force behind this major social change has been fundamental justice. Perhaps equal rights advocates have been satisfied with the strength of this position because difficult questions concerning the substance of black decision making have rarely been asked.

While infrequently posed, these questions are not unimportant. As Pitkin and Peterson have pointed out, the substantive dimension of representation is decision making.[4] In the context of the court, the question becomes whether the special position of the black jurist is also identifiable by decisions systematically related to his or her racial identification. The answer is central to a broader understanding of black elite representation.

Measuring the Decisions of Black Judges

An absolute index of "good" or "quality" judicial decision making has yet to be developed. Instead, a series of relative comparisons is made by examining judges' verdicts and sentences. The first is a comparison of black judicial performance to similar decision making by white jurists. Interracial evaluations are possible because the groups of sixteen black and seventy-five white Metro City judges are responding to similar cases within the same legal, institutional, and community environments.[5]

Judicial decision making may be strongly related to characteristics unique to the presiding judge such as his or her penal philosophy. A second comparison results when the total explanatory power of the individual behavioral differences among the ninety-one jurists is contrasted to the effects of the judges grouped by race. Here the relative importance of the racial factor is established, thus circumventing the difficult problem of determining what constitutes a meaningful disparity. The impact of judicial race on behavior is interpretable as being larger or smaller than the effects of individual differences.

After the decision is made about which comparisons to make (black versus white; race-related versus individual), performance measures are needed. Initially, the relative harshness of judicial sanctions is examined. Behavior is measured both as a percentage of all defendants convicted at bench trials and as the severity of the sentences imposed on convicted offenders. Proprosecution or prodefense behavior means *relatively* high or low conviction rates and *relatively* harsh or lenient sentences.

Next, incorporating data on defendant race, the inter- and intraracial sanctioning of both racial groups and the individual jurists are compared. Here the legal norm of equality of all before the law is explored. Observing how judges convict and sentence defendants of their own and another race may uncover racially motivated behavior among the black and/or white judges— information deemed critical in evaluating judicial performance.[6]

There is a wide range of opinion on the Metro City bench itself about what these comparisons will reveal. Several judges think whites are harsher than blacks. A white judge said, "I suspect the real 'hangers' are exclusively white." In a similar vein, a black observed, "I don't think you'll find black judges being the 'hangers.' I would not be surprised if they were, on average, more lenient." Others believe black judges to be harsher, particularly when sentencing black defendants. "It's said frequently that black judges are tougher on black defendants than white judges are, and my impression is that it's true." This remark by a white jurist tends to be supported by the candid comments of several blacks.

One stated, "I'm not overly sympathetic to the socially or economically disadvantaged defendant argument that one invariably gets." "We are not afraid to give black defendants the sentences they deserve," observed another. "We are not going to deduct anything because the defendant is black. Some of my white colleagues are, I'm afraid, more lenient." Most telling, however, were the problack sentiments expressed by a third black judge.

> I am indeed race conscious but I do try to fight it. When I have a white defendant in front of me, all I hear in the back of my head is 'law and order, law and order,' and the chances are 9 out of 10 that he is going to jail. If there's a black defendant in front of me, I think the chances are 9 out of 10 that he is going to stay out.

A third viewpoint also emerged from the interviews. There was an expectation that individual sentencing differences rather than differences related to judge or defendant race would be most apparent. "I never think of race when I make decisions," a black noted. "I never think, 'I know this black man down the hall who was given a very harsh sentence and I'm going to take it out on this defendant here.' " A black recently appointed to the bench said, "In my relatively brief stay, I would say that sentencing is an individual thing. I do not believe Jews do this or Italians do that or the Irish the other." Finally, the former chief judge emphasized that an individual judge's beliefs, sentencing philosophies, idiosyncracies, and the like are the keys to understanding subsequent behavior. On the subject of race he remarked, "All judges have prejudices and hangups, both black and white. I think on this court you have both black and white Archie Bunkers, racists in other words. But the great majority of them put race behind them when they put on their robes."

Who is correct? Are black judges harsher or more lenient, or is race a poor predictor of sentencing behavior? We can begin to answer these questions by examining verdicts in bench trial cases.

Judicial Determinations of Guilt

Guilty verdicts are returned in nearly 60 percent (59.9 percent) of the 24,100 cases decided in the Metro City trial court. As groups, black judges are below this average and white judges slightly above. Of the 5,328 defendants tried by blacks, 55.5 percent are found guilty while whites return similar verdicts 61.1 percent of the time ($N = 18,772$). The 5.6 percent difference (significance = .001) indicates that black judges are more prodefense than their white colleagues. Because of the large samples, however, the substantive significance of the disparity remains unclear.[7]

Measures of relationship strength appear to minimize its importance. The correlation between type of verdict (dummy variable) and judicial race (dummy variable) is slight—$r = .05$. Controlling for the severity of the cases brought before the groups of black and white judges leaves the relationship unaltered (partial $r = .05$).[8]

Minor disparities in overall conviction rates may conceal larger differences linked to the racial identity of the defendants. Possibly discriminatory behavior might be obscured, for example, if high conviction rates for black defendants were offset by low conviction rates for whites. To determine whether such patterns exist for either group of jurists, inter- and intraracial conviction rates are examined.

Determinations of guilt by race of judge and defendant are displayed in table 4-1. An expectation that judges might favor defendants of their own race finds no support on the black bench. Black judges convict 56.7 percent of the black defendants while finding a bare majority (50.5 percent) of the whites guilty. The interracial disparity (6.2 percent) translates into a weak correlation of $r = .05$ and a partial, controlling for crime severity of .04.

White judges exhibit a pattern similar to their black colleagues' except that the disparity between defendant groups is slightly larger (9.2 percent). Again black defendants are found guilty more often, convicted in 63.0 percent of the

Table 4-1
Determinations of Guilt by Race of Judge and Race of Defendant (Controlled for Crime Severity[a])
(percent guilty)

Black Judges		White Judges	
Black Defendants	White Defendants	Black Defendants	White Defendants
56.7	50.5	63.0	53.8
(4,340)	(988)	(14,955)	(3,817)
Percentage difference = 6.2 Partial $r = .04$[b]		Percentage difference = 9.2 Partial $r = .07$[b]	

[a]Controls are based on the maximum possible sentence for the criminal charge in each case.
[b]Statistically significant at the .001 level.

cases compared to a white guilty rate of 53.8 percent. For this group of jurists, the correlation between race of defendant and case verdict is $r = .09$. Taking into account the varying severity of criminal charges brought against black and white defendants does not change the strength of the relationship significantly (partial $r = .07$).

In comparative terms, black defendants fare poorly at bench trials before either black or white judges. The chances for conviction are greatest for a black defendant appearing before a white judge (63.0 percent). The next highest conviction rate is accorded black defendants before black judges (56.7 percent). Conversely, the greatest opportunity for acquittal lies with white defendants tried before black judges (50.5 percent).

Is this consistently higher conviction rate for black defendants a sign of judicial racism in the Metro City court? The answer remains indefinite at this point. The percentages appear substantial, but the measures of association remain weak. In addition, other case characteristics have been linked to race-related defendant disparities similar to the ones noted here.[9] It is therefore unwise to infer judicial racism from these still sketchy data.

These decision patterns are more informative with regard to the black judiciary; comparative consistency marks the bench trials of black judges. While a disparity between black and white defendants is noted, the difference is of the same magnitude and, more importantly perhaps, in the same direction as the pattern established by white Metro City judges. Both groups of judges convict black defendants more frequently. The behavioral consistency across judicial race becomes even more apparent when the magnitude of individual judicial differences is observed.

Table 4-2 gives the first indication that case outcomes may be influenced

**Table 4-2
Determinations of Guilt by Individual Judge
(Controlled for Crime Severity)**[a]

Defendants Convicted (%)	Number of Judges	Number of Black Judges
80-89	2	0
70-79	15	1
60-69	32	3
50-59	33	9
40-49	7	3
30-39	2	0
20-29	0	0
10-19	0	0
0-9	0	0
	91	16

[a]Mean conviction rate = 59.9 percent.

more by who the particular judge is than by his or her racial identification. In observing the variations in individual conviction rates, a majority of the judges are clustered in the middle range (50 to 69 percent). A number of them, however, diverge substantially. In fact, twenty-six jurists (28.6 percent) are either more than 10 percent higher or lower than the overall average. Within this general distribution, black judges display a similar diversity. Their conviction rates range from a high of 76 percent to a low of 48 percent.

Individual differences are also reflected in the measures of association. The multiple correlation (R) between the 94 category (dummy) judge variable and trial verdict is .17. The multiple-partial, controlling for crime severity, is unchanged. While both coefficients indicate a weak relationship between the presiding judge and a bench trial verdict, these measures of association are significantly stronger (.001) than are those relating judicial race to verdict (r and partial r = .05).

Finally, categorizations by individual judge and defendant race are found in table 4-3. Compared to the disparities previously noted among the groups of black (6.2 percent) and white (9.2 percent) judges (table 4-1), many of the interracial differences appear large. The conviction rates for black and white defendants are less than ten percentage points apart for fewer than half of all Metro City jurists (46.2 percent), and many of the interracial defendant variations are substantial. For twenty judges, the conviction rates between the defendant groups are more than twenty percentage points apart; eleven judges differ by more than 30 percent; and for two the disparity *exceeds* 70 percent. As expected from the previous data, white defendants are the prime beneficiaries. Seventy of the ninety-one jurists establish lower white conviction rates.

Table 4-3
Determinations of Guilt by Individual Judge and by Race of Defendant (Controlled for Crime Severity)[a]

Black Defendants Convicted More Frequently than White			White Defendants Convicted More Frequently than Black		
Percentage Difference	Number of Judges	Number of Black Judges	Percentage Difference	Number of Judges	Number of Black Judges
70-79	2	0	70-79	0	0
60-69	0	0	69-69	0	0
50-59	0	0	50-59	0	0
40-49	2	0	40-49	0	0
30-39	6	1	30-39	1	0
20-29	7	2	20-29	2	1
10-19	25	2	10-19	4	1
0-9	28	6	0-9	14	3
	70	11		21	5

[a]Mean conviction rate = 59.9 percent.

Compared to the more extreme examples of behavior, the verdicts handed down by the individual black judges are not exceptional. Most of their disparities fall within the 0 to 20 range. Eleven black judges convict black defendants more frequently than whites while the remaining five establish the opposite pattern.

In examining behavior at bench trials, black jurists, as a group, are slightly more lenient (prodefense) than their white colleagues. Black judges also convict black defendants more frequently than white defendants. However, the interracial disparity in defendant treatment is comparable in both direction and degree to the pattern displayed by white judges. Of equal importance is evidence that individual behavioral differences are larger than those attributable to judicial race. In fact, determinations of guilt measured either by overall conviction rates or by defendant race are virtually indistinguishable among individual black and white judges in Metro City. Are similar patterns observed elsewhere? That will be determined by examining sentencing behavior.

Sentencing Behavior

The ninety-one jurists in Metro City sentenced 30,350 defendants who either were convicted at trials (bench or jury) or entered guilty pleas. Based on the 93-point severity scale (see chapter 2), the mean sentence for these defendants is 25.5 scale units. The average sentence handed down by the sixteen black jurists is 27.1 scale units ($N = 5,986$). A comparable figure for the white judges is 25.1 ($N = 24,364$). Percentage differences show black judges being 6.2 percent *more* severe than the overall average and white judges 1.5 percent *less* severe. The combined 7.7 percent (2.0 scale unit) disparity is represented by a weak correlation coefficient of .05.

The sentencing difference between the groups of black and white judges is no larger than the variation in trial verdicts. In fact, the only noticeable change is in the direction of the difference. Contrasted to their previous behavior, black judges are slightly more severe (proprosecution) than their white colleagues. This pattern is confirmed when the frequency with which these judges sentence defendants to prison or mete out less serious punishments is examined. Black judges sent 37.4 percent of those they convicted to jail, a figure only marginally greater than the white judge jail rate of 35.6 percent.

After controlling for the maximum possible sentence following conviction, the absolute sentencing difference is reduced to less than 2 percent. The adjusted sentence handed down by black judges is 25.9 scale units (or 1.6 percent above the mean) while the adjusted average for whites is 25.4 (or only 0.4 percent below the mean). The partial correlation between judicial race and sentence, controlling for crime severity, drops to $r = .02$. This weak coefficient along with the minor percentage differences indicates virtually no relationship between judicial race and the severity of criminal sentences.

Both groups of Metro City judges also differ little in their sentencing of black and white defendants. In table 4-4 the average sentences and percentage differences are broken down by race of judge and defendant, again after first adjusting for crime severity. As before, black judicial sentencing is slightly more severe within both defendant groups. Black judges sentence black defendants more harshly than white judges sentence blacks. The same pattern holds in the sentencing of white defendants.

More importantly, however, the interracial defendant disparities within both judicial groups are virtually identical. The average sentence accorded a black defendant by a black Metro City jurist is 18 percent more severe than the average sentence given a white (partial r = .11). The interracial defendant disparity among white judges is nearly the same (19.2 percent; partial r = .14). Along a second dimension then, differences between black and white judges in Metro City are minimal.

As in the analysis of trial verdicts, the contrast between group and individual behavior is marked. In table 4-5 individual sentencing patterns are presented as percentage deviations from the mean sentence (25.5). Again, the figures have been adjusted for the severity of crimes brought before each judge. Over half of the entire Metro City bench (54.9 percent) imposes sentences more than 10 percent above or below the mean. Large disparities are quite common. Sixteen judges are at least 30 percent harsher than the overall average with Metro City's "hanging judge" doling out sentences 95.6 percent above the mean.

Measures of association provide additional evidence emphasizing the relative importance of individual sentencing behavior. The multiple correlation between the trial judge and sentence severity is .35 while the multiple-partial, controlling for crime, is .29. Comparable figures for the impact of judicial race on sentencing are r = .05 and partial r = .02.

Table 4-4
Mean Sentence Severity by Race of Judge and Race of Defendant[a] (Controlled for Crime Severity)

Black Judges		White Judges	
Black Defendants	White Defendants	Black Defendants	White Defendants
27.9	23.3	26.1	21.2
(4,897)	(1,089)	(19,447)	(4,917)
+9.4%	−8.6%	+2.4%	−16.8%
Partial r = .11[b]		Partial r = .14[b]	
Interracial percentage difference = 18.0		Interracial percentage difference = 19.2	

[a]The mean sentence = 25.5 scale units.
[b]Statistically significant at the .001 level.

Table 4-5
Individual Judicial Differences in Sentence Severity—Percentage Deviations from Mean Sentence[a] (Controlled for Crime Severity)

Percentage More Severe	Number of Judges	Number of Black Judges	Percentage Less Severe	Number of Judges	Number of Black Judges
90-99	1	0	90-99	0	0
80-89	0	0	80-89	0	0
70-79	1	0	70-79	0	0
60-69	1	0	60-69	0	0
50-59	1	0	50-59	0	0
40-49	2	0	40-49	0	0
30-39	10	1	30-39	1	0
20-29	3	2	20-29	0	0
10-19	13	1	10-19	17	3
0-9	17	4	0-9	24	5
	49	8		42	8

[a]The mean sentence = 25.5 scale units.

Comparisons by defendant race generally point to the same conclusions (table 4-6); namely, disparities among individual jurists matter much more than race-related behavior. In fact, these large disparities appear to be the general rule rather than the exception. Sixty-four of the ninety-one judges (70.3 percent) mete out sentences *at least* 20 percent harsher to black than to white defendants. For eight judges the interracial difference exceeds 50 percent, and one jurist finds it possible to justify, in his mind at least, sentences for black defendants that are 110 percent more severe than those he gives whites. These figures stand in sharp contrast to the sizable (18 to 19 percent) but nearly identical (1 percent) sentencing disparities found between the black and white benches.

The individual sentencing patterns (tables 4-5 and 4-6) also establish quite convincingly the behavioral diversity among the black judges. Some of their sentencing averages can be classified as harsh, others as lenient, while still others deviate little in either direction from the overall mean. All sixteen blacks mete out harsher sentences to black than white defendants. But even this apparent consistency is deceptive. Individual disparities range from 10 to 65 percent, with 10 to 30 percent sentencing differentials predominating.

The detailed analysis of judicial sentencing behavior does not alter the tentative assessments made earlier. Black and white judges differ little in determining both guilt and the punishment a defendant "deserves" for committing a crime in Metro City. If linked at all, racial differences on the Metro City trial bench can be related to only minor behavioral variations. Race-related defendant disparities appear in sentencing, but a defendant's race makes essentially the *same* difference to both black and white judges.

Finally, individual judicial behavior, while failing to account for all or even

Table 4-6
Mean Sentence Severity by Individual Judge and by Race of Defendant (Controlled for Crime Severity)[a]

Black Defendants Sentenced More Severely than White			White Defendants Sentenced More Severely than Black		
Percentage More Severe	Number of Judges	Number of Black Judges	Percentage More Severe	Percentage of Judges	Number of Black Judges
100-110	1	0	110-110	0	0
90-99	0	0	90-99	0	0
80-89	1	0	80-89	0	0
70-79	0	0	70-79	0	0
60-69	3	1	60-69	0	0
50-59	3	1	50-59	0	0
40-49	6	0	40-49	1	0
30-39	19	2	30-39	0	0
20-29	31	6	20-29	0	0
10-19	22	6	10-19	0	0
0-9	3	0	0-9	1	0
	89	16		2	0

[a]Mean sentence = 25.5 scale units.

most of the disparity in case disposition, is significantly related to both trial verdicts and sentences. More importantly, however, these individual differences have substantially greater impacts on case outcomes than do differences in judicial race—a finding having implications for black elites in general and the black judicial elite in particular.

Black Judicial Decision Making: Some Implications

After its first extensive test, earlier speculation about systematic behavioral differences between the black and white judicial elite remains essentially unsubstantiated. Characterizing the trial bench of a major urban court, only minor variations distinguish the behavior of black and white judges at the critical points where guilt is determined and punishment meted out. This conclusion is strengthened by comparisons to individual differences which emerge as significant over the same collection of criminal cases. For black jurists in Metro City, individuality and heterogeneity characterize their imposition of criminal sanctions.

While this conclusion is both clear and relatively straightforward, some of the implications arising from it are not. Three questions, central to the meaning of black elite representation, deserve consideration. Black judges in Metro City (along with their white colleagues) tend to convict and sentence black

The Decision Making of Black Judges

defendants more often and more harshly than white defendants. Are these defendant disparities evidence of systematic, reverse discrimination on the part of black judges? Second, as a racial group, blacks' decision making is difficult if not impossible to differentiate from white behavior. Do these similarities indicate, as some might argue, that the black Metro City judiciary represents a more traditional and conservative black elite, chosen just for this anticipated behavioral conformity? Finally, it has been posited that a combination of institutional, role, and self-imposed demands frequently pressures black elites to conform to the patterns established by a dominant white elite. Does black judicial decision making represent evidence to support such an assertion?

Concerning the possibility of reverse discrimination, black judges as extremely successful members of their race might conceivably dislike, disdain, and repudiate blacks appearing before them. Sanctioning decisions are obvious tools as their disposal. However, reverse discrimination inspired by this or other possible motives is not supported by these data.

Even though black judges do sanction blacks more severely, the interracial disparity is virtually identical for judges of both races, indicating at a minimum the absence of blatant reverse discrimination. This explanation is not entirely sufficient. Perhaps the entire Metro City bench systematically discriminates against blacks. If so, prejudicial black decision making would just be less visible although not less harmful. To entertain this second conclusion, however, requires accepting as fact the existence of wide-ranging, racist behavior by all but a handful of the ninety-one Metro City judges.

This issue is examined from the defendant's perspective in the following chapter. After including other case and defendant characteristics that would have added undesired complexity here, most of the racial difference in defendant treatment is either related or inferred to be related to nonracial and sometimes nondiscriminatory factors (for example, pretrial detention status, type of defense counsel, prior criminal record). While not legitimizing disparities attributable to these legal and extralegal variables, the subsequent analysis accounts for much of the disparity that simply appears here as a gross or absolute black-white defendant difference. In conjunction, both chapters indicate that black Metro City jurists, while not necessarily free from individual bias, in all likelihood do not systematically discriminate against the black defendants appearing before them.

Does the similarity between black and white behavior signify black elite conformity? The question is as difficult to answer with certainty as it is important. This subject is often raised or implied when the distinction is made between "traditional" and "second-generation" black elites.[10] A traditional black elite is viewed as representing a conservative, nonthreatening black leadership frequently exploited by a dominant white elite. Conformity to white decision-making patterns is the hypothesized behavioral norm. This group is contrasted to a younger (or at least more recent) "second generation" of black leadership. Individuals in this category are seen as reform-minded, activist in orientation, and more likely to articulate the interests of the politically, economically, and socially disadvantaged black American.

The issue of conformity goes beyond the "typing" of black leadership. Some argue that black conformity may result from individual, institutional, or environmental demands or pressures.[11] To win acceptance, black elites have been accused of adopting the dominant, middle-class value system with its inherent bias toward the status quo. A well-recognized socialization process within the legal profession makes such behavior even more likely in the case of black judges. According to one black jurist, the result is co-optation. "No matter how 'liberal' black judges may believe themselves to be, the law remains essentially a conservative doctrine, and those who practice it conform. Judges who are black tend to keep a low profile ... they strive not to rock the boat...."[12] This tendency, compounded by external pressures such as close scrutiny by public officials or a lack of cooperation from white colleagues, may mean conformity is the path of least resistance.

As evident in chapter 3, both the black and white benches appear to have been carefully chosen from the establishment center of the legal profession in the city. Resulting from tight party control over the process of judicial selection, judicial backgrounds and careers, regardless of race, are characterized by high-quality educations, government legal service, prestige law firm affiliations, and extensive civic and professional activity. These attributes do not describe a cross section of the legal fraternity. Descriptively at least, the court overrepresents both the "traditional" black and white legal establishments.

Behaviorally, however, individual jurists of both races demonstrate substantial diversity. Perhaps the diversity is less than a more representative selection from the entire legal community would produce. Nevertheless, even among these restricted groups of black and white jurists, behavior is not consistent in a single direction, be it liberal or conservative, proprosecution or prodefense, harsh or lenient.

Perhaps considered a traditional black elite based on their past experiences, by their behavior the black judiciary does not represent a particular judicial mindset. Instead, black judges act as individuals. Their decisions demonstrate marked diversity—a diversity that includes severity and leniency and, in all probability, competence, incompetence, wisdom, and ignorance.

These findings may disappoint those who believe that black elite representation should be translated into preferential treatment. Equal justice in the legal order dictates otherwise. In attempting to alleviate past inequities, one could hardly justify either favoritism or reverse discrimination. This does not mean that blacks fail to fulfill other dimensions of a unique judicial role. Black jurists in Metro City and elsewhere may act symbolically as positive representatives to and of their race and substantively as educators and reformers. This analysis, however, suggests the need to distinguish between the nonsanctioning roles of black judges and their actual decision making. It has been stated that black judicial representation is needed to avoid distorting the entire legal system.[13] In Metro City this distortion is absent and so is the equally dangerous one of behavior based on the racial identity of the presiding judge.

Notes

1. For example, see E. Franklin Frazier, *Black Bourgeois* (Glencoe, Ill.: Free Press, 1957); James Q. Wilson, *Negro Politics: The Search for Leadership* (Glencoe, Ill.: Free Press, 1960); David H. Howard, "An Exploratory Study of Attitudes of Negro Professionals toward Competition with Whites," *Social Forces* 45 (September 1966):20-27; Lester M. Salamon, "Leadership and Modernization: The Emerging Black Political Elite in the American South," *Journal of Politics* 35 (August 1973):615-645; Lucius Barker and Jesse McCorry, *Black Americans and the Political System* (Cambridge, Mass.: Winthrop Publishers, Inc., 1976).

2. To the extent they exist, most analyses of black decisionmakers have been narrowly defined case studies or individual leadership portraits. See Roosevelt Johnson, "Black Administrators and Higher Education," in *Black Political Life in the United States,* ed. Lenneal Henderson (San Francisco: Chandler Publishing Company, 1972), pp. 200-214; Tilman C. Cothran and William Phillips, Jr., "Negro Leadership in a Crisis Situation," *Phylon* 22 (Summer 1961):107-118.

3. Stuart Nagel, "Ethnic Affiliations and Judicial Propensities," *Journal of Politics* 24 (February 1962):95.

4. Hanna Pitkin, *The Concept of Representation* (Berkeley: University of California Press, 1967); Paul E. Peterson, "Forms of Representation: Participation of the Poor in Community Action Programs," *American Political Science Review* 64 (June 1970):491-507.

5. Four white judges who did not hand down at least twenty-five verdicts and twenty-five sentences have been omitted from this analysis.

6. Maurice Rosenberg, "The Qualities of Justices—Are They Strainable?" *Texas Law Review* 44 (June 1966):1079; Charles F. Stafford, "The Public's View of the Judicial Role," *Judicature* 52 (August/September 1968):77.

7. To avoid overlooking possibly important crime-specific behavior patterns, the more general analysis discussed presently was replicated within the individual crime categories. The results of this investigation confirmed the findings reported here.

8. The control variable is the statutory maximum sentence that could possibly have been imposed upon conviction (measured in years).

9. John Hagan, "Extra-Legal Attributes and Criminal Sentencing: An Assessment of a Sociological Viewpoint," *Law and Society Review* 8 (Spring 1974):357-383.

10. Joyce Gelb, "Blacks, Blocs, and Ballots: The Relevance of Party Politics to the Negro," *Polity* 3 (Fall 1970):45-69; Salamon, "Leadership and Modernization."

11. Harold Baron, "Black Powerlessness in Chicago," *Transaction* 6 (November 1968):27-33.

12. Bruce McM. Wright, "A Black Brood on Black Judges," *Judicature* 57 (June/July 1973):360-365.

13. Fannie Klein of the Institute of Judicial Administration quoted in Lawrence Mosher, "Few Blacks Make the Bench," *National Observer,* December 1, 1969, p. 26.

5 The Defendant's Perspective: Conviction and Sentencing of Black Defendants

Since the late 1920s controversy has existed over the degree and importance of race-related disparities in the criminal case disposition process. Social scientists have explored a wide variety of local legal systems to determine whether black and other minority group defendants receive harsher treatment than their white counterparts and, if so, whether this differential treatment can be considered discriminatory.[1] Notwithstanding the difficulties inherent in this field of study, work persists for one simple but compelling reason.[2] To the extent that it exists, discriminatory sanctioning represents a fundamental distortion of the ideal of equal justice for all before the law.

This chapter continues research in this area by investigating the decisions meted out to 34,258 black and 9,344 white defendants appearing in the Metro City trial court. Initially, conviction rates and sentence severity are contrasted by defendant race. An even more challenging task is then to interpret the interracial differences and similarities that emerge. The challenge results both from the complexity of the criminal justice process and from divergent explanations for race-related disparities uncovered elsewhere.

In an attempt to incorporate these judicial complexities and competing theories in a realistic assessment of the defendant race question, a causal model of the disposition process has been developed. Including additional case characteristics, this model is operationalized using path analytic techniques to determine the relative impact of various legal and extralegal components of the race-disposition relationship. From this analysis we are in a better position to conclude whether discrimination is evident or whether racial disparities result from legally justifiable distinctions among defendants.

The issue of primary concern here may have been voiced most eloquently by Frederick Douglass. Speaking in 1883, he stated,

> Justice is often painted with bandaged eyes, she is described in forensic eloquence as utterly blind to wealth or poverty, high or low, white or black, but a mask of iron however thick could never blind American justice when a black man happens to be on trial.[3]

Here a judicial system is on trial as we investigate the truth of Douglass' assertion as it pertains to the Metro City court.

Interracial Disparities—Absolute Differences

In studies measuring race-related sanctioning, absolute disparities nearly always favor whites.[4] Frequently restated in other ways, Henry Allen Bullock's comment describes the issue in its broadest terms: "It is generally concluded that Negroes receive differential treatment in arrest, sentencing, and imprisonment. . . ."[5] The research focus is narrower here, but the testable hypotheses remain. We may expect Metro City blacks to be found guilty and sent to jail more often and also to receive harsher sentences than white offenders.

The first type of case disposition examined is the decision to convict or acquit. Sanctioning patterns may relate to the type of crime committed. To explore this possibility, sixteen divergent crime categories are examined individually. In four of the sixteen, white defendants are found guilty more often than blacks (table 5-1). The largest absolute disparity remains under 2.5 percent. This difference is not statistically significant, and neither are the three remaining disparities which are even smaller. In twelve other crime categories, black defendants are convicted more frequently than whites. Many of these disparities are also slight; seven crimes have interracial differences of less than 5 percent while four others manifest moderate disparities of between 5 and 10 percent. In only three instances are the interracial differences statistically significant.

Examining conviction rates over all 43,602 felony cases supports a tentative conclusion that we have tapped at most a small interracial disparity.[6] White defendants ($N = 9,344$) are found guilty 72.0 percent of the time while blacks receive guilty dispositions in 75.9 percent of 34,258 cases. With a sample this large the difference is, of course, statistically significant and in the hypothesized direction. Yet the importance of a 4 percent disparity remains an open question. For the present it is considered as meaningful but marginal with a final evaluation deferred until possible explanatory factors are evaluated.

There is far less maneuverability in assessing interracial differences in jail rates; convicted black defendants are sentenced to prison substantially more often than whites. Table 5-2 reveals the breadth and consistency of the pattern. In fifteen crimes blacks are recipients of jail terms more frequently; and in the remaining crime, gambling, blacks are only slightly favored. Over all cases, jail sentences are meted out to only 19.6 percent of the convicted white offenders compared to 40.2 percent of the convicted blacks. In the Metro City criminal court, blacks are twice as likely to go to prison as whites.

Considering the positioning of the jail/no jail dichotomy within the sentence severity scale, it is not surprising that black defendants also receive harsher sentences of all types. Blacks average more severe punishments in fifteen of the sixteen crime categories (table 5-3). With two exceptions (manslaughter and delinquency of a minor), crimes that manifest large interracial jail disparities also tend to be associated with sizable overall sentencing differentials; the same relationship holds in categories where the disparities are smaller. Averaging over

Table 5-1
Percentage of Defendants Convicted by Race in Selected Crime Categories

Crime Category	Black Defendants	White Defendants	Percentage Difference	r
Murder	80.0 (1,015)	77.9 (86)	+2.1	.01
Manslaughter	87.5 (361)	80.6 (72)	+6.9	.07
Robbery	73.8 (4,855)	75.7 (395)	−1.9	−.01
Aggravated assault	71.1 (2,464)	66.2 (497)	+4.9	.04
Minor assault	76.0 (1,917)	75.6 (761)	+0.4	.00
Burglary	76.9 (5,789)	75.6 (1,727)	+1.3	.01
Larceny	80.1 (3,138)	81.9 (753)	−1.8	−.02
Automobile larceny	82.1 (378)	84.4 (77)	−2.3	−.04
Stolen property	86.8 (2,028)	83.9 (601)	+2.9	.03
Forgery-counterfeiting	84.9 (755)	81.2 (309)	+3.7	.04
Rape—serious sex	64.4 (742)	66.0 (144)	−1.6	.01
Drug offenses	71.0 (4,553)	66.2 (1,634)	+4.8	.05[a]
Weapons offenses	76.6 (2,685)	67.1 (377)	+9.5	.07[a]
Driving under the influence	73.4 (1,088)	57.2 (327)	+16.2	.16[a]
Gambling	56.6 (258)	48.7 (156)	+7.9	.07
Contributing to delinquency	78.7 (207)	73.6 (174)	+5.1	.05

[a]Statistically significant at .01 level.

all cases, white defendants receive mean sentences of 19.9 scale units while blacks average sentences of 26.4 units. This 6.5-unit difference translates into a correlation coefficient equaling .16, which is comparable to the interracial disparity in jail rates ($r = .17$).

In Metro City we find similar absolute disparities in prison rates and sentence severity. Along both measures blacks are punished more severely than

Table 5-2
Percentage of Defendants Jailed by Race in Selected Crime Categories

Crime Category	Black Defendants	White Defendants	Percentage Difference	r
Murder	85.8 (812)	82.1 (67)	+3.7	.02
Manslaughter	52.8 (316)	50.0 (58)	+2.8	.01
Robbery	71.1 (3,582)	46.8 (299)	+24.3	.14a
Aggravated assault	40.2 (1,751)	25.2 (329)	+15.0	.11a
Minor assault	30.6 (1,456)	13.7 (575)	+16.9	.17a
Burglary	46.7 (4,451)	25.3 (1,305)	+21.4	.18a
Larceny	36.3 (2,515)	18.2 (617)	+18.1	.15a
Automobile larceny	29.8 (299)	23.1 (65)	+6.7	.05
Stolen property	31.0 (1,761)	18.7 (504)	+12.3	.11a
Forgery-counterfeiting	19.0 (641)	16.3 (251)	+2.7	.03
Rape–serious sex	57.9 (478)	41.1 (95)	+16.8	.12a
Drug offenses	23.0 (3,232)	11.1 (1,082)	+11.9	.13a
Weapons offenses	28.7 (2,056)	17.8 (253)	+10.9	.08a
Driving under the influence	7.6 (799)	2.4 (327)	+5.2	.09a
Gambling	4.8 (146)	5.3 (76)	−0.5	−.01
Contributing to delinquency	30.1 (163)	15.6 (128)	+14.5	.16a

aStatistically significant at the .01 level.

whites with most of the differences appearing substantial. The evidence is less clear as far as determinations of guilt or innocence are concerned. Marginal differences mark most of the defendant race-conviction relationships. These disparities may be interpreted as being significant, but the argument is more difficult to make. In light of these findings it seems necessary to group race-related jail and sentencing disparities and to distinguish them from conviction rates.

Table 5-3
Mean Sentence Severity by Race in Selected Crime Categories[a]

Crime Category	Black Defendants	White Defendants	Unit Difference	r
Murder	66.5 (812)	61.9 (67)	+4.6	.05
Manslaughter	36.5 (316)	31.4 (58)	+5.1	.10
Robbery	40.6 (3,582)	33.1 (299)	+7.5	.11[b]
Aggravated assault	26.4 (1,751)	23.0 (329)	+3.4	.09[b]
Minor assault	19.0 (1,456)	15.0 (575)	+4.0	.17[b]
Burglary	26.9 (4,451)	23.5 (1,305)	+3.4	.12[b]
Larceny	22.6 (2,515)	19.7 (617)	+2.9	.12[b]
Automobile larceny	20.4 (299)	18.1 (65)	+2.3	.08
Stolen property	22.0 (1,761)	19.5 (504)	+2.5	.10[b]
Forgery-counterfeiting	20.8 (641)	20.3 (251)	+0.5	.02
Rape—serious sex	37.9 (478)	29.1 (95)	+8.8	.15[b]
Drug offenses	20.2 (3,232)	17.0 (1,082)	+3.2	.14[b]
Weapons offenses	19.0 (2,056)	17.0 (253)	+2.0	.07[b]
Driving under the influence	11.9 (799)	8.8 (327)	+3.1	.16[b]
Gambling	8.8 (146)	9.6 (76)	−0.8	−.05
Contributing to delinquency	20.7 (163)	19.2 (128)	+1.5	.07

[a]Mean sentence based on 93-point sentence severity scale.
[b]Statistically significant at .01 level.

We have carefully avoided labeling any relationship discriminatory. Absolute race-related disparities exist, but at present we cannot conclude more. Caution is in order because other explanations have been advanced to account for similar differences found elsewhere. After these initial disparities are charted, the difficult and challenging task of interpretation remains.

Interpreting Interracial Disparities—A General Path Model

Alternative explanations for interracial disparities are directly attributable to the inherent complexity of the case disposition process. Believing the direct link between race and sanctioning oversimplifies a multifaceted relationship, researchers have incorporated intervening variables into broader analyses of the question. In general, these are attempts to view case decisions in more comprehensive terms by including several variables, of which race is only one.

These efforts represent notable advancements in exploring the impact of race in adjudicatory proceedings. Complex interrelationships among a series of variables describe the reality of the process. While we give full credit to these studies, frequently they, too, are limited. Restricted by either missing variables or a narrow theoretical focus, many fail to examine the full range of explanatory alternatives. To mitigate this problem, it is useful to develop a more general race-disposition model unencumbered either by limitations on the available data or by a favored explanatory theory.

An approach to constructing this model is to introduce and define a network of direct and indirect causal relationships between defendant race and case outcomes. The principles of path analysis are applicable to such a complex causal structure.[7] Specifically, a multistage, multivariate, recursive path model enables us to explicitly state theoretical propositions and to describe potential "pathways of influence" linking race and disposition decisions.

This elaboration is more than an intellectual exercise. We need to interpret the disparities found in Metro City. Within the framework of a general model, we can make explicit omissions because of data limitations. Not every explanatory option can be explored, but at least we can specify where gaps remain. Finally, the general model is useful in theory building by functioning as a convenient reference in developing alternative theoretical structures and/or analytic approaches.

A recent critic of sanctioning studies concluded that nearly every project was incomplete, fragmentary, and " . . . necessarily inadequate to the question at issue."[8] Beginning with a general model and then operationalizing it within the limitations imposed by the data represents a comprehensive approach to analyzing an emotionally charged issue, set in a complex environment and already subject to a variety of interpretations.

Criminality Component

Edward Green is one of the strongest and most persuasive advocates of what will be referred to as the criminality component of the race-disposition model.[9] Green contends that while absolute race-related disparities exist, most likely they are the indirect result of differing patterns of criminal behavior. Some subsequent research has supported his contention.[10] According to Green, "When the effect of these variant patterns of criminal behavior is controlled . . . the differences in the severity of the sentences [by defendant race] become negligible."[11] Here the defendant race-case disposition relationship is indirectly operative through various determinants of criminality (see figure 5-1).

The factors most frequently used to gauge criminality are a defendant's prior record and the severity of the criminal act that has been committed. In Green's studies black defendants not only had more extensive prior criminal records but also committed more serious offenses.[12] Similar patterns are evident elsewhere as absolute race-disposition relationships vanish when criminality variables are controlled.[13]

When race acts through differences in criminality, it is argued that resulting disparities are legitimate and even necessary responses to legally relevant and justifiable distinctions among cases. "Yes, blacks are treated severely in terms of sentencing," observed a white Metro City judge, "but the reasons seem to me to be based on more extensive criminal records and more serious crime. If a person has a long record, white or black, he will get the 'appropriate' sentence." This indirect linkage is not considered discriminatory; blacks are sanctioned more harshly because of the greater extent of their criminal activity.[14] "There is no overt discrimination," a court administrator concurred. "Most of what happens in terms of higher sentencing can be attributed to the more serious previous records on the part of black defendants." Bluntly stated, proponents of the criminality component of a general race-disposition model contend that if blacks receive harsher punishment as a result of committing more serious crimes or committing crimes more frequently, they are receiving only their due.

Class/Status Component

An interpretation of race-related disparities giving primary emphasis to legally relevant criteria presents the criminal justice mechanism in a favorable light. Alternative explanations are far less complimentary. Links between race and wealth or class differences among defendants may affect dispositions. Labeled the class/status component of the general model, this explanatory alternative

Figure 5-1. Criminality Component.

posits that inequities arise as middle- and upper-class defendants receive more favorable treatment in the criminal justice process than do their lower-class counterparts. Differential impacts can be hypothesized to be both direct and indirect. Class and status differences affect case outcomes as well as a series of important intermediate decisions (for example, bail/bond proceedings, plea negotiations). Racial disparities emerge to the extent that black and other minority group members are poor and lower class or are so perceived by criminal justice decisionmakers. The class/status component is depicted in figure 5-2.

Specifically, defendant race and class status can be related with whites generally perceived as predominantly middle and upper class and blacks predominantly lower class. Again blacks are expected to fare worse than whites in the criminal justice process. The disparity is attributed, in part, to income differentials between poorer blacks and more affluent whites.[15] But more than poverty is operative. Stuart Nagel sees the indigent facing "... the handicap that he is and looks lower class while those who determine his destiny ... are middle class."[16] So in addition to the tangible burdens of poverty, the poor black confronts a criminal justice mechanism that may more readily, or perhaps only, identify with and respond equitably to economically privileged defendants.

One effect of this race-class relationship may be a direct impact on dispositions. A white Metro City judge unwittingly revealed such a bias. "On average, white defendants have more of an opportunity to break out of the crime cycle with a supportive environment than blacks. Therefore, their chances of repeating are less, and I may have taken that into account in sentencing. But I don't consider that racism."[17] As figure 5-2 indicates, the effect may also be indirect and operate through one or more predisposition decisions that ultimately affect case outcome. For example, class differences among defendants have been found related to representation by private counsel, favorable bail determinations, and successful plea negotiations—decisions subsequently linked to differential sanctioning.[18] "It's largely a chicken and egg question," observed another white judge. "Most black defendants are also poor and it's hard to figure out in terms of types of crimes or the adequacy of defense counsel whether it's economics that results in harsh punishment or race. My feeling is that a lot of it is economics."

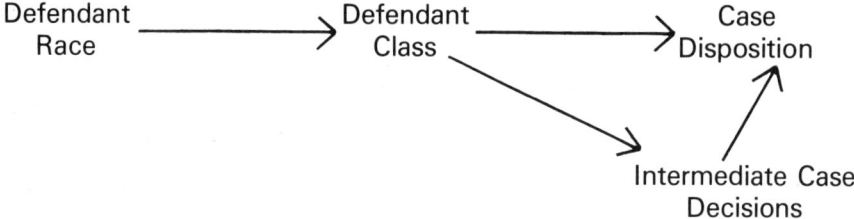

Figure 5-2. Class/Status Component.

The Defendant's Perspective

Like the criminality component, the class/status interpretation proposes no direct race-disposition linkage. This is their only point in common, because the general thrust and implications arising from each differ markedly. It may be argued that race-related disparities are acceptable when associated with legal criteria. One would be hard-pressed, however, to justify disparities that are tied to class and income differences among defendants. Thus, to the extent that it can be supported by actual data, the class/status dimension represents injustice that is operative in the criminal process. The inequities described, although related to race, are filtered through class disparities; as such, this component of the general model can be distinguished from both the criminality linkage already described and the explanatory path we have yet to discuss—"pure" racism.

Racism Component

Race-related sanctioning disparities both exist and usually result in less favorable treatment for black defendants. This finding is frequently made by those whose subsequent interpretations make them advocates of either the criminality or class/status component of the general model. For some, however, these data are ample proof that racism directed against black Americans is commonplace in criminal case dispositions.[19] For example, Wolfgang and Reidel conclude that, "Far from being 'freakish' or capricious ... the significant racial differentials found in the imposition of the death penalty are indeed produced by racial discrimination."[20]

Several, but by no means all, Metro City black judges concur in this view. One remarked, "I think there is a significant amount of racial discrimination in this court. You would still find more serious sentences for blacks even if you could somehow remove the effect of individual case circumstances." Another said rhetorically, "Go to the prisons and you will see a prison population 90 to 95 percent black. Can you tell me there isn't some racism if we only commit 60 percent of the crimes?" Finally, a third commented, "There are some judges who sentence blacks on things they wouldn't sentence whites on, and I don't think there's any question that this is a fairly widespread problem."

Thus, a third and perhaps the most ominous interpretation of the absolute disparities is posited. To the extent that race-related differences appear, they are hypothesized to result from racist or discriminatory behavior on the part of the key decisionmakers. Depicted in figure 5-3, this component of the general model is viewed as a clear and direct relationship linking racial differences to case outcomes; the minority group defendant is victimized by unfavorable decisions based solely on his or her race.

Proponents of the racism explanation usually do not attack alternative interpretations, but they often ignore or fail to test them. It is now evident how misleading these omissions might be. Figure 5-4 depicts the three major components of the race-disposition model. When we also include possible

Defendant Race ⟶ Case Disposition

Figure 5-3. Racism Component.

linkages between the criminality and class/status components, we see that labeling absolute differences as racist is only one of three or more viable explanations for the disparities uncovered.[21] One can interpret as racist only that portion of the association not accounted for by the criminality and class/status components. The same approach is required in interpreting the other two explanatory paths. Each one could be *the* major determinant of the race-related disparities, but their impacts can be gauged accurately only after the influence of the other factors is evaluated.

Having described the model in general form, we are in a position to operationalize it within the context of the Metro City court. To do this will entail simplifying assumptions and limitations. Nonetheless, even a limited test of the model will provide useful insights into the relative influences of its three principal components and allow them to be examined jointly.

Interpreting Interracial Disparities—A Path Analytic Approach

Path analysis appears well suited to the interpretive task outlined.[22] By specifying simple and compound pathways of influence between defendant race and sanctioning, the technique allows us to observe the relative strengths of the

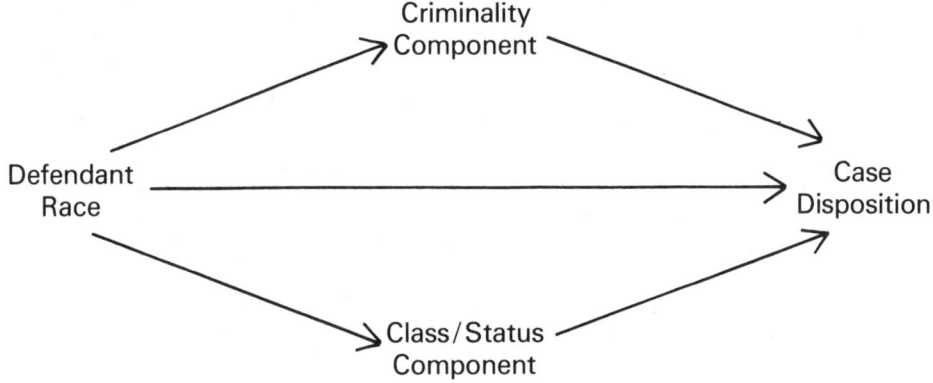

Figure 5-4. General Race-Disposition Model.

The Defendant's Perspective

racism, criminality, and class/status components evident in Metro City.[23] Before proceeding, however, we must meet or approximate the required statistical assumptions.[24]

Of immediate concern is the assumption in path analysis that residuals or error terms not be correlated among themselves or with more than one variable in the causal system. To approximate this, all relevant variables should be specified in the model. In the operational version, a defendant's prior record and class/status do not appear, raising the prospect of correlated residuals. These unmeasured variables create a regrettable but unavoidable loss of information. Their absence, however, does not undermine the rest of the analysis.

The effects of defendant socioeconomic status (SES) and prior record are merged with the impact of racial differences. Figures 5-5 and 5-6 describe the situation in simplified form. In figure 5-5 we specify the direct effect of race on dispositions as path *a* and indirect effects via defendant SES (path $b \times c$) and defendant prior record ($d \times e$). This figure describes the original path model. Figure 5-6 represents the operational version where SES and prior record remain unmeasured. The race-disposition relationship now includes both the direct and indirect effects of race. Therefore, what we will measure as a race impact is really an *upper bound* for racial influences that also include class and prior-record effects. These variables are not eliminated from the causal system and do not become correlated residuals. Instead, they may be conceived of as "phantom" variables whose influences are merged with that of race.

Of the numerous models that could be developed from these data, only a general defendant race-*sentencing* path model is actually operationalized.[25] In addition to race and sentence severity, other case characteristics are utilized. They include severity of the criminal charges, total number of charges, bail amount, pretrial bail status, type of defense counsel, method of case disposition, and evidence of charge reduction. These variables are summarized in table 5-4.[26]

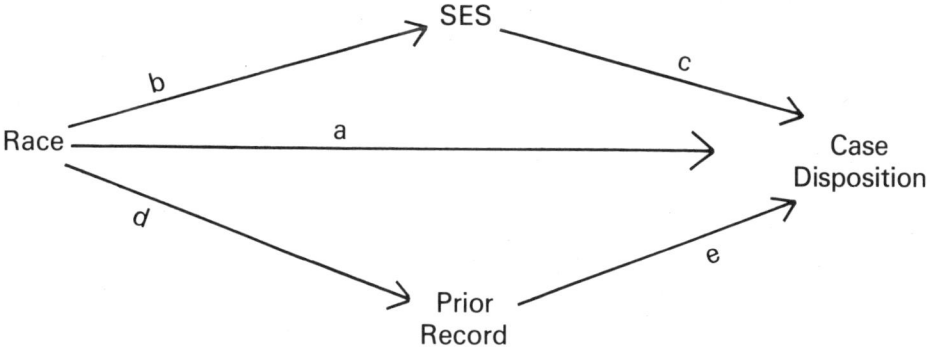

Figure 5-5. Race-Disposition Model Including SES and Prior Record.

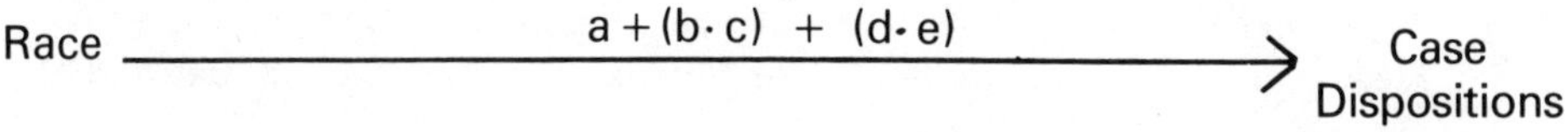

Race ─────────── a + (b·c) + (d·e) ──────────→ Case Dispositions

Figure 5-6. Race-Disposition Model where SES and Prior Record Remain Unmeasured.

In the analysis, we first briefly survey a fully defined or "just identified" model and from it construct a more easily interpreted and parsimonious reduced version based on the strongest simple and compound paths linking race and sentencing outcomes. Path coefficients in the reduced model are then reestimated to gauge the impact of the remaining pathways. At this point we are able to compare the relative contributions made by the three major components of the general model in explaining the absolute disparities observed previously.

Fully Defined Model

Figure 5-7 depicts the fully defined race-sentencing path model for the Metro City court. For ease of reference, individual variables are numbered in causal sequence, and the figure is presented along with a summary table (table 5-5) describing the operationalization in detail. The simple correlations among the variables in the model appear as appendix B.

The total defendant race-sentence correlation is $r = .16$. We hypothesize race

Table 5-4
Independent Variables Included in the Path Analysis

Variable Name	Description
Charge severity	Maximum possible sentence (in years) for each charge (311) in sample
Number of charges	Total number of charges originally lodged against defendant
Bail amount	A dollar amount indicating bail requirement
Bail status	Defendant's pretrial status, either pretrial release or detention
Defense counsel	Legal representation by either court-appointed counsel (public defender or court-appointed private counsel) or private, retained counsel
Method of disposition	Case disposed by either guilty plea or trial (judge or jury)
Evidence of charge reduction	Sentencing on either the most serious charge originally lodged or a charge less than the most serious

The Defendant's Perspective   89

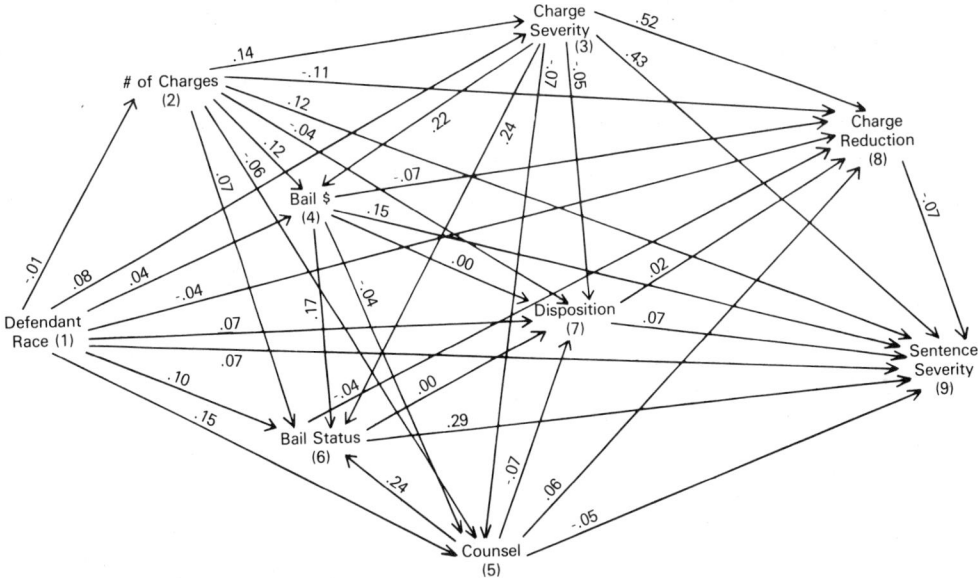

[a] All path coefficients larger than .00 are statistically significant at the .01 level.
Figure 5-7. A Fully Defined Race-Sentencing Path Model.[a]

(1) as having a direct effect on sentencing outcomes (9), p_{91}, in addition to indirect effects through the criminality and class/status components. Portions of both components are examined. The number of charges (2) and charge severity (3) represent the extensiveness and seriousness of the criminal behavior alleged (criminality component). Bail amount (4), type of counsel (5), bail status (6), disposition (7), and charge reduction (8) describe intermediate decisions or institutional responses that may differentially affect various defendant groups (class/status component). Relationships are hypothesized between defendant race and the criminality and the class/status components, between elements of the criminality and the class/status components themselves, among individual factors within each component, and between each variable and sentence outcome.

The model as described is really too complex to analyze in detail, but some general observations are in order. Lending credibility to the entire model is evidence that the direction and magnitude of the most frequently described paths are in accord with prior research.

Within the criminality component positive relationships exist between the number of charges and eventual sentence (p_{92} = .12) and charge severity and sentence severity (p_{93} = .43). The extent of alleged criminal activity can also be expected to influence intermediate decisions (class/status). The number of

Table 5-5
Variables Included in the Race-Sentencing Path Model

Variable	Code-Description
Race of defendant (1)	1 = black defendant 0 = white defendant
Number of charges lodged against defendant (2)	
Maximum potential sentence for charge/crime (3)	measured in years
Amount of bail (4)	measured in dollars
Type of defense counsel (5)	1 = court-appointed public or private defender 0 = retained counsel
Defendant pretrial bail status (6)	1 = pretrial detention 0 = pretrial release
Disposition (7)	1 = judge or jury guilty verdict 0 = guilty plea
Charge reduction—evidence of plea negotiation (8)	1 = sentenced on most serious charge or charge tied as most serious 0 = sentenced on less than most serious charge
Sentence severity (9)	93-point sentence severity scale (see chapter 2)

charges is positively related to both bail amounts ($p_{42} = .12$) and bail status ($p_{62} = .07$). The charge severity-bond paths are substantially stronger ($p_{43} = .22$ and $p_{63} = .24$). The more serious the alleged offense, the higher the bail requirement and the less likely the defendant is to obtain pretrial release.

Logical relationships also link the number of charges to both charge severity and charge reduction. Charging a defendant with more offenses increases both the prospect that at least one of the charged offenses will be serious ($p_{32} = .14$) and the likelihood of eventual sentencing on a reduced charge ($p_{82} = -.11$). Finally, the strong, positive path between charge severity and charge reduction ($p_{83} = .52$) indicates that reduced charges are much less likely to be given in more serious and perhaps more visible cases.

Bail amount and bail status are both interpreted as intermediate stages in the disposition process that may affect final case outcome directly or indirectly through the plea bargaining process. Only direct effects materialize. Higher bail amounts are related to more severe sentences. The marked dropoff ($p_{94} = .15$) from the simple correlation ($r_{49} = .35$) indicates that part of the impact of bail amount on sentence severity operates through a defendant's pretrial bail status. This interpretation is supported as we observe a significant relationship between bail amount and bail status ($p_{64} = .17$) and also find an important path linking bail status and sentencing ($p_{96} = .29$). The latter relationship concurs with previous studies indicating that harsher sanctions are more likely to be accorded defendants unable to win pretrial release.

The remaining class/status variables yield a mixed set of relationships with sentencing outcomes. The generally accepted notion that the criminal justice system rewards those who cooperate and punishes those who do not receives some support. A defendant whose case proceeds to trial does, indeed, wind up with a higher average sentence ($p_{97} = .07$). The path between charge reduction and sentence ($p_{98} = -.07$) indicates that in cases where charges are reduced relatively more severe sentences are meted out. With crime severity held constant, defendants convicted on a reduced charge are more likely to be sentenced closer to the maximum on the reduced charge while those convicted on more serious charges tend to be given less than maximum sentences. Plea "bargains" in Metro City may be more apparent than real.

One of the few relationships running counter to general expectations links type of defense counsel to sentence severity. In Metro City, defendants represented by court-appointed counsel receive less severe sentences than do defendants with privately retained counsel ($p_{95} = -.05$). While a similar finding has been reported elsewhere,[27] the pattern contradicts the notion that private counsel are more successful advocates.

The path marks one of the few exceptions to a broad range of relationships that are close to previously observed patterns. Therefore, the operational path model appears to be a realistic portrayal of a complex network of interrelationships among critical variables in the disposition process. The paths from defendant race to other variables in the causal system provide further evidence in this regard while also demonstrating support for the three major components of the general model.

Despite a marginal path to the number-of-charges variable ($p_{21} = -.01$), the criminality explanation is evident as black defendants are convicted of more serious offenses than are whites ($p_{31} = .08$). The class/status component is also in evidence with blacks more frequently recipients of unfavorable intermediate disposition decisions. They are given higher bail ($p_{41} = .04$), are less likely to obtain pretrial release ($p_{61} = .10$), are more likely to go to trial ($p_{71} = .07$), and are more likely to be represented by court-appointed counsel ($p_{51} = .15$). Even their apparent advantage in charge reduction ($p_{81} = -.04$) is largely eliminated by harsher sentences on reduced charges.

Finally, the racism component is left. After the effects of portions of the criminality and class/status interpretations are removed, a significant, direct race-related disparity remains. The path coefficient ($p_{91} = .07$) may confirm charges that behavior most accurately termed racist exists in the sanctioning process. This conclusion still must be guarded because the direct race-sentencing path may include the unmeasured effects of defendant class/status and prior record.

Reduced Model

Interpreting the impact of defendant race within the context of the fully defined model is a difficult task at best. It is hard to gauge the relative impacts of the criminality and class/status components or identify the specific, indirect paths that are most important in each. Well over fifty individual pathways can be followed linking defendant race to sentence outcome. Since most of these compound paths contribute extremely little to the total race-sentencing association, it becomes useful to construct a more parsimonious model.

The goal in developing this reduced model is the retention of the strongest simple and compound paths of influence between defendant race and sentencing outcomes. The standard to be used is not simply the size of the paths emanating from race or flowing into sentencing, but rather the total impact of a particular pathway, derived by multiplying the individual coefficients that comprise the path. This was done for every compound path. No standard measure of significance is available in determining which pathways to keep and which to discard, but a reasonable cutoff did emerge.[28] Remembering that the sum of all possible paths is .16 (equaling the simple correlation between race and sentence severity), we decided that compound paths of less than .01 would be too weak to be considered theoretically meaningful. After the weak paths were eliminated, three compound paths and three intervening variables remained in addition to the direct race-sentencing relationship. Figure 5-8 depicts the reduced model including reestimated path coefficients.

This version describes in much clearer fashion the key linkages between defendant race and sentencing outcomes. The three intervening variables represent two of the primary components of the general race model with the direct path representing the third. Table 5-6 presents the individual pathways and their relative strengths in the model.

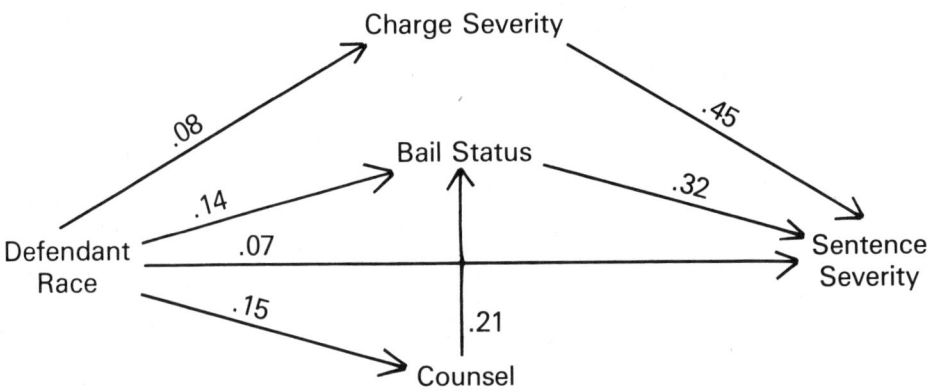

Figure 5-8. A Reduced Race-Sentencing Path Model.

Table 5-6
Reduced Race-Sentencing Model—Significant Pathways of Influence

Pathway and Component	Path Coefficients and Products	Percentage of Total Relationship
Criminality		
Race → Charge → Sentence	(.08)(.45) = .036	22.4
Class/Status		
Race → Bail status → Sentence	(.14)(.32) = .045	28.0
Race → Counsel → Bail status → Sentence	(.15)(.21)(.32) = .010	6.2
		34.2
Racism		
Race → Sentence	.07	43.5
	Total correlation = .161	100.0%

The criminality component is described by charge severity and shows blacks receiving more severe punishment, in part at least, because they are charged with more serious offenses. The path from charge to sentence is clearly the strongest in the model, but the path from race is the weakest. The product of both (.036) amounts to 22 percent of the total race-sentencing relationship. This is less than either of the two remaining components.

Class/status is depicted by two paths. Both include a defendant's pretrial bail status as an intervening variable with one also incorporating type of defense counsel. The race-counsel-bail status-sentence linkage is the weakest in the reduced model, accounting for about 6 percent of the observed disparity. It indicates that black defendants are more likely to be represented by court-appointed counsel. These attorneys appear less effective than privately retained counsel at getting defendants released pending trial. The bail status disparity is also linked directly to racial differences. Black defendants are less likely to make bail and be released, with the compound path of .045 representing nearly 28 percent of the total racial difference. Both paths describe inequities because the direct consequence of pretrial detention status is harsher sentencing.

Bail status unquestionably emerges as the key class/status variable in the model. Besides being unjust punishment if the defendant is later found innocent, prisoner status may create negative impressions among court officials as well as result in decreased opportunities to prepare a defense. Thus, blacks are indeed disadvantaged to the extent that they are less likely to make bail. We are probably witnessing race-related inequities caused primarily by the limited financial resources of Metro City blacks. Being poorer than their white counterparts, blacks are less able to retain private counsel and, more importantly, less able to raise the bail that has been set. While this pattern is more class-related than racist, it clearly describes a disturbing inequity in the criminal justice mechanism.

The last path connecting defendant race to sentence outcome is the direct one between the two variables. With a coefficient equaling .07, it accounts for over 40 percent of the total association. This component has been labeled racist; and except for the unmeasured, intervening influence of defendant prior record and SES, no other interpretation is tenable. After the influence of both the criminality and class/status variables is taken out, race-related differences in sentencing severity remain.

Conclusions

The reduced model allows us to reach some tentative conclusions in interpreting the absolute race-sentencing relationship noted previously. The actual pathways of influence between race and sentence outcome do approximate the major components of the general path model. This means that while proponents of a criminality interpretation are correct in advocating the inclusion of legally relevant variables, greater criminality by blacks does not emerge as the sole explanation for the disparities reported. Also, the criminal justice mechanism responds, by either conscious design or circumstance, to defendants favored by private counsel and pretrial release status. On the average, white defendants are the primary recipients of these favorable institutional responses which later affect sentencing. Finally, all the observed race-related disparities cannot be "explained away" by using either the criminality or the class/status explanations. The largest proportion of the total race-sentencing relationship may describe unjustified, discriminatory treatment.

In light of the available evidence, defendant race makes meaningful differences in case disposition. These differences are significant and unjust to the extent they operate through a class-oriented institutional structure or result directly from discriminatory decisions on the part of key decisionmakers. Considerable caution, however, must be exercised in entertaining this conclusion. Care is needed because of major differences in the impact of defendant race on conviction rates and sentence severity. A priori, there is no reason why one would hypothesize behavior labeled as discriminatory occurring at one point in the highly interrelated disposition process and not the next; one would expect that discrimination is either present or absent. Therefore, the finding that racism may exist in sentencing while racial disparities are minimal in determinations of guilt leads us to suggest an alternative explanation.

The answer may be found in the varying impact of a defendant's prior criminal record on these two disposition decisions. As previously noted, prior record and sentence severity have often been found strongly and positively related. On the other hand, the relationship between record and case verdict should be minimal, given that information on prior record is not usually in evidence at trial.[29] Juxtaposing our findings and the conventional wisdom regarding prior record encourages speculation that record, not defendant race, may be responsible for a major portion of the absolute disparity left unexplained by the other independent variables. Likewise, the small race-related disparities in conviction rates may simply reflect the minimal influence of prior record on this sanctioning decision. This interpretation is offered as a reasonable but untested alternative and must remain so until prior record can be investigated in conjunction with the variables examined here.

Perhaps widespread racial discrimination is not to be found in the Metro City trial court. Such a conclusion would not surprise a few of the blacks who preside there. Representative are the following comments: "I suppose some racial discrimination exists but there's nothing glaring. I have three colleagues in mind who are bad judges. They're unfair, but they're unfair to both black and white defendants." Another remarked, "Discrimination is not too bad; only in a very few instances have I become aware of problems."

Such sanguine appraisals must still be treated very cautiously. Subtle forms of discrimination may still exist (see chapter 6). Even "small" disparities at any point quickly become major inequities if repeated. Also, the trial court remains but one stage among many in the overall case disposition process. So while blatant discrimination may not be evident, racism cannot be conclusively ruled out in this court or elsewhere in the city's criminal justice system.

Notes

1. Most of the major race-case disposition studies are cited in John Hagan, "Extra-Legal Attributes and Criminal Sentencing: An Assessment of a Sociological Viewpoint," *Law and Society Review* 8 (Spring 1974):375-383 and James L. Gibson, "Race as a Determinant of Criminal Sentences: A Methodological Critique and a Case Study," *Law and Society Review* 12 (Spring 1978):455-478.

2. For a discussion of some of these problems, see Stuart Nagel and Marian Neef, "Racial Disparities that Supposedly Do Not Exist: Some Pitfalls in the Analysis of Court Records," *Notre Dame Lawyer* (October 1976):87-94.

3. Frederick Douglass as quoted in A. Leon Higgenbotham, "The Black Lawyer in America Today," *Harvard Law School Bulletin* 22 (February 1971):57.

4. See the sources cited in Hagan, "Extra-Legal Atrributes," and Gibson, "Race as a Determinant of Criminal Sentences." As we shall see, many of these studies do part ways over either the size of the disparity or its interpretation.

A few exceptions to this general pattern exist. See Dean Jaros and Robert I. Mendelsohn, "The Judicial Role and Sentencing Behavior," *Midwest Journal of Political Science* 11 (1967):471-488; Robert M. Terry, "The Screening of Juvenile Offenders," *Journal of Criminal Law, Criminology and Police Science* 58 (1967):173-181.

5. Henry Allen Bullock, "Significance of the Racial Factor in the Length of Prison Sentences," *Journal of Criminal Law, Criminology and Police Science* 52 (November/December 1961):412.

6. These cases are the population of validly coded felony records in the Metro City data and include, in addition to the sixteen crimes analyzed separately, fifteen less common felonies.

7. Donald E. Stokes, "Compound Paths: An Expository Note," *American Journal of Political Science* 18 (February 1974):191-214; Kenneth C. Land, "Principles of Path Analysis," in *Sociological Methodology 1969*, ed. Edgar F. Borgatta (San Francisco: Jossey-Bass, 1969), pp. 3-37.

8. Hagan, "Extra-Legal Attributes," p. 379.

9. Edward Green, *Judicial Attitudes in Sentencing* (New York: St. Martin's Press, 1961), pp. 56-63.

10. See, for example, Hagan, "Extra-Legal Attributes," p. 379; Lawrence P. Tiffany et al., "A Statistical Analysis of Sentencing in Federal Courts: Defendants Convicted after Trial, 1967-1968," *Journal of Legal Studies* 4 (June 1975): 369-390; Maureen Mileski, "Courtroom Encounters: An Observation Study of a Lower Criminal Court," *Law and Society Review* 5 (May 1971):505-510; Robert M. Terry, "Discrimination in the Handling of Juvenile Offenders by Social-Control Agencies," *Journal of Research in Crime and Delinquency* 4 (July 1967):227-228.

11. Green, *Judicial Attitudes in Sentencing*, p. 63.

12. Edward Green, "Inter- and Intra-Racial Crime Relative to Sentencing," *Journal of Criminal Law, Criminology and Police Science* 105 (September 1964):348-358; Green, *Judicial Attitudes in Sentencing*, pp. 56-63.

13. See note 10.

14. One important caveat is in order. The criminality component of the race-disposition model is characterized as nondiscriminatory, but inequities exist to the extent that blacks are more frequently arrested and/or victimized by overcharging.

15. Stuart Nagel is the most persuasive proponent of this view. See his *Legal Process from a Behavioral Perspective* (Homewood, Ill.: Dorsey Press, 1969), pp. 87-95. See also Stephen Bing and S. Stephen Rosenfeld, "The Quality of Justice: In the Lower Courts of Metropolitan Boston," *Criminal Law Bulletin* 7 (June 1971):398; and William J. Chambliss and Robert B. Seidman, *Law, Order and Power* (Reading, Mass.: Addison-Wesley Publishing Company, Inc., 1971).

16. Stuart Nagel, "The Tipped Scales of American Justice," in *The Politics of Local Justice*, eds. James R. Klonoski and Robert I. Mendelsohn (Boston: Little, Brown and Company, 1970), p. 120.

17. See also William J. Chambliss, *Crime and the Legal Process* (New York: McGraw-Hill Book Company, 1969), p. 294; and Patricia M. Wald, "Poverty and Criminal Justice," in *The Criminal in the Arms of the Law*, eds. Leon

Radzinowicz and Marvin E. Wolfgang (New York: Basic Books, 1971), pp. 582-614.

18. Research on these questions is steadily increasing. See, for example, Anne Rankin, "The Effect of Pre-Trial Detention," *New York University Law Review* 39 (June 1964):641-655; David N. Atkinson and Dale A. Neuman, "Judicial Attitudes and Defendant Attributes: Some Consequences for Municipal Court Decision-Making," *Journal of Public Law* 19 (1970):69-87; Nagel, *Legal Process from a Behavioral Perspective,* pp. 87-92.

19. The sophistication of these projects varies widely, with some studies controlling for nonracial factors and others not. See Bullock, "Significance of the Racial Factor," p. 412; Southern Regional Council, *Race Makes the Difference: An Analysis of Sentence Disparity among Black and White Offenders in Southern Prisons* (Atlanta: Southern Regional Council, 1969); Marvin E. Wolfgang, Arlene Kelly, and Hans C. Nolde, "Comparison of the Executed and the Commuted among Admissions to Death Row," *Journal of Criminal Law, Criminology and Police Science* 53 (1962):301-311; Richard Quinney, *The Social Reality of Crime* (Boston: Little, Brown and Company, 1970), p. 220.

20. Marvin E. Wolfgang and Marc Reidel, "Race, Judicial Discretion and the Death Penalty," *Annals of the American Academy of Political and Social Science* 407 (May 1973):133.

21. A natural time sequence structures the expected pathways of influence between the criminality and class/status components of the model. Defendant class/status preceded a defendant's prior record, and both were established before the current crime was committed and intermediate (and possibly class-related) decisions were made. Figure 5-9 displays the hypothesized interconnections between the two criminality (prior record, crime severity) and two class/status (defendant class/status, intermediate case decisions) factors.

22. For more detailed treatments of the subject, see Stokes, "Compound Paths"; Land, "Principles of Path Analysis"; Fred Kerlinger and Elazar Pedhazur, *Multiple Regression in Behavioral Research* (New York: Holt, Rinehart and

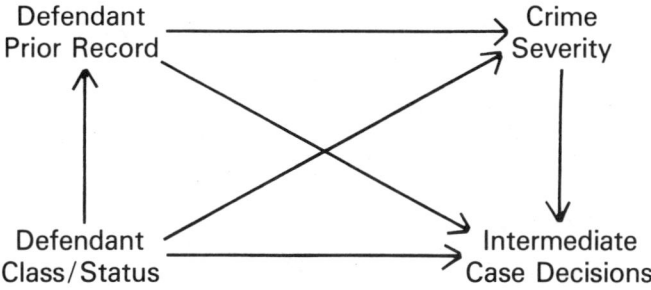

Figure 5-9. Criminality and Class/Status Linkages.

Winston, 1973); Samuel A. Kirkpatrick, *Quantitative Analysis of Political Data* (Columbus, Ohio: Charles E. Merrill Books, Inc., 1974); Hubert M. Blalock, Jr., *Causal Models in the Social Sciences* (Chicago: Aldine Publishing, 1971).

23. Using this technique, we are able to partition a correlation between variables in the path model into alternative pathways of influence. With variables expressed in standard scores (z), a path coefficient (p_{ij}) can be derived that is the standardized regression coefficient (Beta weight) obtained from ordinary least-squares analysis and measures the fraction of the standard deviation of an endogenous (dependent) variable for which a particular independent variable is directly responsible. Correlation coefficients can, therefore, be broken down into simple and compound paths with each segment in a diagram or term in a structural equation representing the product of the elementary path coefficient linking the individual steps in a unique pathway.

For example, in the three-variable case (figure 5-10), $r_{13} = p_{31} + p_{32}p_{21}$, where $p_{31} = \beta_{31.2}$, $p_{32} = \beta_{32.1}$, and $p_{21} = r_{12}$. The first term (p_{31}) is the simple path coefficient (standardized beta) between V_3 and V_1 indicating the direct effect of 1 on 3. The second term, the compound path $p_{32}p_{21}$, measures the indirect impact of V_1 on V_3 acting through the intervening variable V_2. The sum of the simple and compound pathways describes the total association (correlation) between V_1 and V_3 but in a form that makes meaningful distinctions among patterns of influence.

24. The appropriateness and validity of the technique rely on meeting or approximating a rather strict set of assumptions. Two meriting special attention are the assumed existence of causal relationships and the assumed absence of reciprocal causation. The absence of reciprocal causation, also called the recursiveness assumption, means that the causal flow is unidirectional, thus eliminating feedback loops.

Although feedback can never be ruled out entirely or causality proved conclusively, an important contributing factor in meeting these assumptions is the presence of natural time intervals between events. Time sequences imply causal ordering, thereby lessening the chances for feedback. Natural time intervals are present in both the general path model outlined and the Metro City data on which the operational version is based.

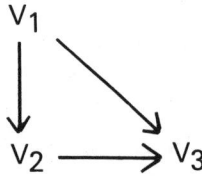

Figure 5-10. Three-Variable Path Model.

The Defendant's Perspective

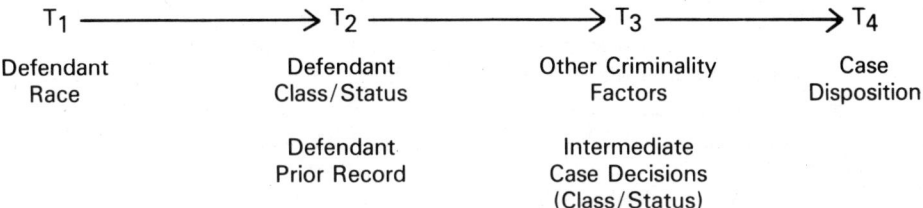

Figure 5-11. Time Sequences in the General Race-Disposition Model.

The time sequences for the general model are illustrated in figure 5-11. The main components of the race-disposition model are divided into four time periods that correspond to the occurrence of events in the life of a defendant and the history of this particular criminal case. Clearly a defendant's racial identity, the variable whose impact we want to chart, is established first in the causal sequence. Nothing in our system determines race, thus making it an exogenous variable.

The second time period (T_2) begins after birth and ends just prior to the commission of the criminal act under consideration. Variables of importance included within it are the criminality component factor, prior record, and the class/status component, defendant class/status. While some may argue that race and SES are so interrelated as to render them virtually indistinguishable, class cannot cause race. Prior record falls in the latter stages of time period 2 and is subject to the influences of both defendant race and class/status. All three factors clearly precede the events in period 3.

The variables falling in the third time frame (T_3) encompass the elements of the criminal case under consideration prior to final disposition decisions on guilt and sentencing. A logical time sequence can be established within this period as cases flow from arrest to arraignment to adjudication. The extent and seriousness of the criminal act(s) are determined at arrest or early in case proceedings. Following closely are intermediate decisions on counsel type and bail amounts. Then just prior to final case disposition, plea bargaining and charge reduction may occur. Finally, sanctioning outcomes in T_4 are viewed as causally dependent directly and indirectly upon one, several, or all the variables that have proceeded them in T_1, T_2, and T_3.

Other assumptions are those required in regression analysis. Interval levels of measurement are assumed using interval variables, "dummy" variables, and an approximated interval sentence severity scale. Because of the large sample size, normal distributions can be assumed. Minimal measurement error is assumed to result from accurate coding and a rigorous case deletion policy. In instances where a complex causal model has been developed, usually certain simplifying assumptions have been necessary. The two that are made here are the appropriateness of both a linear and an additive path model. For a more elaborate discussion of these assumptions, see citations in note 22.

25. This initial effort will focus on a full sample of cases with attempts to operationalize crime-specific models deferred at present. Large samples are advantageous in path analysis, and working with a wide variety of criminal charges increases the potential utility of the findings. Conviction rates are not analyzed because the interracial disparity is small in relation to sentence and jail disparities. Sentence outcomes are selected over jail rates because path analysis has usually been employed in research where interval dependent variables are available. Omission of the jail/no jail dichotomy is acceptable; at nearly every point of comparison, interracial sentence severity and jail rate disparities approximate each other.

26. Missing data were deleted pairwise or variable by variable. Because of the case deletion criteria adopted there were no missing data for the charge severity, number-of-charges, or method-of-disposition variables. Missing data on bail amounts included 18.1 percent of the cases where defendants remained in pretrial custody with no dollar bail established. Instead of setting arbitrary dollar figures in these cases, they were omitted in bail calculations. In determining bail status, the 2.3 percent of the defendants classified as "fugitives" were also treated as missing. Valid defense counsel codes appeared in 98.9 percent of the cases. Cases containing only a single charge were classified as missing on the evidence of charge reduction variable.

27. Peter Greenwood et al., *Prosecution of Adult Felony Defendants in Los Angeles County: A Policy Perspective* (Santa Monica, Calif.: The Rand Corporation, 1973), p. vii.

28. Land, "Principles of Path Analysis," pp. 34-35.

29. While information on prior record does not come out directly at trial, the indirect effect may be substantial. Prior record may affect predisposition decisions (such as the amount of bail), which in turn can influence ultimate case outcome.

6 Where Do We Go From Here?

The uncertain interpretation of defendant disparities underscores the need for additional research on race issues in the legal process. To date, every investigation has had shortcomings, many of which were unavoidable. Poorly kept criminal records, uncooperative court officials, methodological difficulties, and financial constraints have led to a variety of research problems; too few defendants, judges, or crimes may be examined in too few jurisdictions over too short a time. With little likelihood of a comprehensive assessment of either judge or defendant race questions in the offing, future efforts will be most valuable to the extent they are able to examine questions previous studies have left partially or totally unanswered. In the course of this inquiry, several important issues have been raised that are worthy of further exploration.

Several judges and court officials mentioned that discrimination against black defendants may exist in the Metro City court but not appear on the computerized records. They were referring to subtle courtroom practices and procedures that place minority group defendants at a disadvantage. A black judge noted, "I would characterize the discrimination here more as favoritism toward whites that is not extended toward blacks." More revealing was the comment of a white court administrator:

> I really don't think blacks are treated the same way as whites in this court. For example, public defenders are not considered "real" lawyers by some, and as a result blacks with public defender advocates are treated differently in a couple of ways. Their cases usually go to trial last, and judges do not take defense arguments as seriously. Small things happen that add up.

How widespread are these less obvious biases in Metro City and elsewhere? How do they operate and what are their cumulative effects on case dispositions?

There is a need to supplement detailed analyses of case histories with more sensitive indicators of court activity. By themselves, observational studies are not entirely satisfactory. While they may pinpoint significant behavioral patterns not evident in court records, they are unable to measure dispositional inequities in sufficient breadth. A combination of research techniques is required. Whenever possible, an examination of a large number of case records should be combined with an in-depth exploration of black and white defendants' dispositional histories, using random samples drawn from the original data sets. At present, even though obvious bias was not evident in the Metro City data, discrimination in all aspects of trial court activity cannot be ruled out conclusively.

A greater effort should also be made to disentangle the effects of defendant race and socioeconomic status. The path model was only partially successful in this regard because specific indicators of class or status were missing. Detailed information such as income or employment history for relatively small samples or summary census tract measures for larger data sets would enable the relative importance of race to be more precisely contrasted to that of SES in determining case outcome. Both explanatory alternatives could then be compared to the influences of legally relevant and extralegal case characteristics such as prior record and pretrial bail status.

Another significant extension in this line of research would be to incorporate information on the race of the victim when appropriate. Preliminary work indicates that disposition patterns for black defendants may vary significantly depending on both the nature of the crime and whether the victim was white.[1] Blacks may be punished more harshly for crossing the color barrier in committing crimes or, conversely, be given lighter sentences when convicted of intraracial offenses and offenses viewed as commonplace within the black community. Do these patterns of inter- and intraracial punishment remain even after the effects of other case and defendant characteristics have been held constant?

One indication that they may exist in Metro City can be inferred from the comments of a white judge:

> Another important consideration in sentencing seems to be the attitudes we have about the lifestyles of the defendants we sentence. Sometimes we tend to accept the brutality and violence that take place in the black community. Our attitude is that this kind of stuff is a way of life. We think, "He only was in the hospital four or five hours" or "He only had 23 stitches," and therefore, we tend to go lighter on defendants convicted of crimes that lead to this result that we would have if these crimes had been committed in an upper-class or middle-class neighborhood.

Clearly, the sentencing implications of protectionist attitudes toward the white community and paternalistic attitudes toward the black community deserve further exploration.

To this point, unanswered questions and suggestions for future research have centered on the trial court. Because trial court proceedings take place relatively late in the disposition process, inequities appearing at earlier stages may go undetected in analyses of verdicts and sentences. The arraignment court in Metro City and lower courts in other jurisdictions serve important screening functions for their respective trial courts. In Metro City, this court conducts preliminary hearings and preindictment probation proceedings, both possibly leading to early as well as favorable case dispositions; in fact, over 40 percent of all felony defendants have charges against them dismissed or are placed on probation as the result of rulings in the arraignment court. Their partnership with the trial court and their independent decision-making authority mean that lower courts must also be investigated for possible discriminatory defendant treatment. A comprehensive assessment of racism in the entire adjudication stage of any criminal justice system with a lower court, including, of course, Metro City, cannot be completed until this is done.

Additionally, there is some reason to believe that race-related inequities are more likely to be found in lower courts. Generally, they are subject to less scrutiny by the media, civil rights activists, and the black community than are trial courts; often these court observers do not view "preliminary" proceedings as being as important to ultimate case outcomes as actual trials. Infrequent public scrutiny may be coupled with judges' and prosecutors' impressions that lower court rulings are not visible and are unlikely to be appealed. The result may be that personal prejudices are given freer reign. Does this situation accurately describe the Metro City arraignment court? While a definitive answer is the goal of ongoing research, one black trial court judge did remark that discrimination was indeed likely to appear in the arraignment court as favoritism in case dismissal for white defendants and for defendants represented by private attorneys.

The decision-making and background analyses of the black bench have also left important questions unanswered. The unique contributions and special responsibilities of black judges within the courtroom and community were catalogued in chapter 1. Presented by articulate spokesmen for the black judiciary, this listing amounts to a persuasive argument for increasing black judicial representation. Do less visible and vocal black judges also see themselves as accepting additional responsibilities and an atypical judicial role? Some tentative assessments can be derived from judicial interviews in Metro City.

The black judge is an important symbol of hope and encouragement for the disadvantaged, according to black advocates. The black judges interviewed indicated an awareness of their symbolic role. Several believe they represent positive models of success and achievement to black youth whom they meet either in or out of court. One black female judge cited the example of a girl who had heard the judge speak to her high school graduating class and that single encounter had inspired her to a career in the law. With evident pride she noted that the girl is now an assistant U.S. attorney. Another black judge acts as an informal advisor and confidant to black law students in the area. At the time of the interview, four or five students appeared to have virtually taken up residence in his office. When asked about the gathering, he replied, "It's very important for these kids to know that blacks who have already made it want them to make it too."

The symbolic benefits of the black judiciary are not viewed as being restricted exclusively to black youth. "Our existence has got to lead to increased confidence in the system by all minorities," a third black judge commented.

Another said, "I think it makes a hell of a lot of difference when you look up and see a black face on the bench. It has a beneficial psychological impact on black lawyers as well as black defendants."

Despite the importance these judges attach to their presence, symbolic representation requires little effort. Do these judges also actively articulate black interests? Have they established a dialogue with their white colleagues concerning racial issues or acted in other ways as reformers within the court or community? Their answers to these questions diverge somewhat from the claims made by vocal black judges in other jurisdictions.

Black and white judges agree that relatively little communication takes place among judges on the Metro City bench about race, or anything else for that matter. The former chief judge remarked, "I don't think there has been any real discussion of the black experience or a heightening of sensitivity." A black recalled, "In my many years on the bench, we have never really discussed race among ourselves or with our white brothers." Logistical and time constraints appear to have inhibited collegial interaction in part. Judges' chambers and courtrooms are widely scattered throughout a mammoth city hall building. Judges repeatedly made reference to the size of the bench and docket as reasons why discussions on all issues were so infrequent. Moreover, several judges indicated that extensive communication is not to be expected inasmuch as judgeships are essentially solitary positions. However, these explanations may not be sufficient. Nowhere in the interviews did black judges mention that a dialogue with their white colleagues about race was an important or necessary responsibility for them to assume. Perhaps obstacles to communication discouraged this dialogue, but no one referred to this frustration explicitly.

The reform spirit among these judges is also more circumscribed than what might be anticipated from the writings of other black judges. The primary difference is that Metro City blacks limit their advocacy of black interests almost exclusively to noncourt settings. The only exception was a black woman judge who was instrumental in increasing employment opportunities for blacks in service-related jobs within the court. When asked about her apparently unusual activism, she remarked pointedly, "We can't continue to let it be a white man's world until it's time to collect the garbage." Other than this example, black judges did not indicate any action taken while serving in a *judicial* capacity that would distinguish them from their white colleagues.

Their judgeships, however, have helped many of them gain access to visible, nonjudicial positions where their views on racial issues were freely expressed. Memberships on various federal, state, and local boards and commissions were mentioned frequently. Some of these were policy-making posts, and others were honorary; some were law-related and others not. For example, one judge recalled his experience as a member of the state crime commission where he successfully channeled more LEAA money for new equipment to police precincts serving predominantly black residential neighborhoods. Another said, "Off the bench, I think my obligation is to be a change agent within the community in any number of ways, to suggest programs that are needed and to change bad programs into good ones."

Why do black judges in Metro City generally exclude race-conscious activism when they don their robes? Two possibilities present themselves. First, scrutiny by white judges, the media, and party leaders may contribute to a reluctance by blacks to express any views on race issues in an official capacity. Their small numbers may make them sensitive to their visibility within the community. As a result, they might refrain from activism within the court because they are apprehensive that any reform efforts will quickly lead to criticism that could damage their careers and actually hinder positive change.

Second, Metro City black jurists as a group may not wish to violate role constraints which they see as prohibiting the advocacy of any special interest, racial or otherwise. In other words, they may have strong opinions on racial matters but not voice them in a legal setting because they believe it to be inappropriate judicial behavior. While the underlying causes differ, the consequences of both explanations are similar. External constraints and/or self-imposed restraints would effectively limit black judicial activism. Is either interpretation approximated in Metro City?

A thorough review of the court administrator's newspaper clipping file for the 1968-1974 period did not indicate that black judges received an undue amount of press attention. Occasionally the presiding judge in a notorious case was the subject of extensive coverage in the city's newspapers. Less frequently, a particular sentence was criticized editorially as being too lenient given the facts of a case. But this attention and infrequent criticism did not involve black judges a disproportionate number of times.

White judges and court administrators concurred with this conclusion. A white judge said, "A double standard and extra scrutiny for blacks? I haven't noticed this. They are given respect and regard based on their individual abilities." In fact, several believe that if any external constraints exist, they evolve from the black community as pressure to be more responsive to black interests. For example, a court administrator remarked, "Some black judges appear frightened of the criticism they will receive if they don't go along with the interests of the black community at large."

When these issues were raised with the black judges, none acknowledged being pressured by the black community and some were quite critical of the attention paid them by whites. "Black judges are in a fish bowl," said one black judge. Another observed, "For every criticism leveled against a black judge I can show you a white who is also guilty but who hasn't been criticized. The reason is that we are visible. Every black who is a judge walks on egg shells. You learn that lesson early or you don't survive." Others, however, differed and did not believe that a double standard existed. An older black woman observed, "No, I haven't noticed any undue criticism or review, either personally or among my black colleagues." Based on these preliminary findings, the black judges in Metro City do not appear to be operating under the type of intense scrutiny that has been noted by black jurists elsewhere.[2] External pressure is in evidence, but it is most likely not greater for blacks than whites and by itself probably not sufficient to have silenced otherwise activist judges.

Perhaps the role orientations and attitudes of these judges precluded their advocating race-related reforms in nonadjudicatory capacities on the bench. First, chapter 3 found these judges to be atypically successful and talented, even when measured against the most exacting judicial recruitment standards. Their achievements within Metro City's legal establishment may make them reluctant to criticize it. Second, their strict adherence to legal norms, such as total impartiality, may also stem from a socialization process that began in law school. Thus, high recruitment standards and the traditional legal values embraced by those chosen may have resulted in a black bench in the 1968-1974 era that was primarily status quo-oriented.

For the moment, direct evidence to support this assessment is scant. However, both black and white judges commented on the unusual characteristics of the black bench at this time. Several compared black judges selected in the post-1964 period to those studied here. The chief judge said, "I think the early blacks were much better than the blacks we have today. They were really pioneers. They had to be good, and they were good." More indirect but equally revealing was the comment by a veteran black jurist: "On the whole, I think the bench in Metro City today is less qualified than it was in the early 1970s."

Other comments indicated the black bench to be predominantly middle to upper class in background and to possess judicial qualifications exceeding their white colleagues'. "Black judges serving at that time were primarily 'patrician' blacks," observed a white court administrator. A candid black said, "I learned to be middle class when I was in law school." Concerning their qualifications, another black judge remarked, "Man for man, woman for woman, the black bench is head and shoulders above the white bench." A third continued, "To get here a black person has to be pretty good. A white person might get here with lesser talent." Do having exceptional qualifications and middle-class or upper-class values mean the black judges examined are not likely to be activist on the bench? Perhaps. If so, Wilson's description of black "prestige leaders"[3] or Judge Wright's belief that black judges keep a "low profile"[4] might be more appropriate than the image portrayed by Judge Crockett of a crusading black judiciary.

Regardless of which characterization is closer to reality, these judges are not pawns in the hands of the white legal establishment. Unlike blacks who have been given impressive-sounding titles without corresponding authority, "window dressing" positions according to Johnson,[5] these judges have the capability to bring about change. As a group, they appear to be activists off the bench, but their attitudes and judicial role perceptions may prevent them from displaying their views in either sanctioning or nonsanctioning behavior on the bench.

Several judges' comments indicate that a so-called second generation of black judges may be emerging that does not possess extraordinary qualifications. If this is so, exploring differences in backgrounds, philosophies, and decision making between groups of black judges should become an important part of future black judicial research. All black judges descriptively represent the black community, but only some will articulate the most pressing law-related concerns of blacks. What characterizes those most likely to provide substantive as well as descriptive representation and, just as importantly, to provide representation that respects the unique nature and function of courts in society?

This final point deserves emphasis. A judge's chambers and court must be distinguished from political backrooms and legislative assemblies. The special responsibility of courts to resolve disputes impartially means that racial partisanship in many, if not all, aspects of judicial service will be inappropriate. The black judges in Metro City appear sensitive to this role constraint. Perhaps their distinction between activism on and off the bench is indeed most appropriate given the positions they hold. How much further could black judges go in pressing for change in an official capacity without jeopardizing their integrity as judges? This issue should become an integral part of subsequent evaluations of the black bench. In spite of disclaimers to the contrary, it may not be easy to be an outspoken black advocate on the bench without giving the impression of being a racial partisan or actually responding to racial factors in rendering decisions.

One of the most heartening findings in this analysis has been the behavioral diversity of the black bench. The individuality that characterizes black judges' sentencing should do much to reassure skeptics who feared that substantive black decision-making authority would be used to avenge past injustices. This could not have happened systematically here because their decisions, in all manner of cases, were so disparate. It remains to be seen whether recent additions to the black bench in Metro City or black judges elsewhere are also able to distinguish activism either on or off the bench from favoritism in their decision making.

A direct way of increasing black power and influence in society is to get blacks into positions of authority within political, social, and economic institutions of consequence. After years of relative indifference to courts as a political institution of importance, black community leaders are beginning to make concerted efforts to influence judicial selection. In Metro City a judicial recruitment panel has been established by the local chapter of the National Bar Association to screen candidates and then work for the election of those whom it endorses. The panel's influence remained symbolic prior to 1974. Subsequently its support has become increasingly important for black as well as white candidates in both party primaries and general elections. Political party endorsements are still necessary for black judicial success. But indications of an increasingly independent black electorate coupled with a black leadership sensitive to the importance of judicial power may create a new route to the bench for blacks in Metro City. Should black judges be chosen primarily with the backing of black voters, a third, unique group of black judges would be installed. Attitudinal and behavioral research would then need to be extended to include comparisons between these newly elected and more independent blacks and "first-" and "second-generation" black judges selected with the blessings of white politicians.

Judicial attitudes and role perceptions need to be explored much more systematically and comprehensively than they have been here. The views of a subset of the Metro City bench permit preliminary assessments at best. In addition, it will become increasingly important to detail specific linkages between attitudes and behavior in investigating complex issues surrounding black judicial representation.

Black judges are expected to satisfy conflicting demands from different groups in the community, demands that are meant to affect both their decisional and their nondecisional responsibilities. Some blacks expect them to be advocates, and others look to them for inspiration. The legal community anticipates that as judges they will adhere closely to legal norms and also be fair-minded and efficient arbiters. And whites watch black judges warily, some fearing and some hoping they will abuse their power.

On the whole, black judges in Metro City have withstood these pressures well. While not satisfying every demand, they have articulated black interests without antagonizing those who might differ with them. More importantly, they appear to have inspired confidence as judges within both the black and the white communities without dispensing favors. Now we need to evaluate how black judges in other courts at other times have met these challenges.

Although more is known about racism in trial courts, research on black defendant treatment must continue for other reasons. The complexities of the disposition process require that efforts be made to investigate every adjudicatory stage with greater precision. Also, the lack of consensus on the extent or very existence of racial discrimination in criminal case dispositions may mean that no general conclusion is possible; factors unique to each jurisdiction may be determinative. If this is so, the research effort becomes more difficult but no less important.

This book will not reassure those looking for easy answers to the racial issues studied. Discrimination in Metro City was not obvious and judicial behavior not predictable along racial lines. The exploration of the black judiciary is just beginning at a time when analyses of racial disparities in defendant treatment are being extended to lower courts. While frustrating and difficult, work in these areas is not without significant rewards, because in determining how racial differences among judges and defendants influence court proceedings, broader questions of justice and equal opportunity in the U.S. legal process are also being examined.

Notes

1. Henry Allen Bullock, "Significance of the Racial Factor in the Length of Prison Sentences," *Journal of Criminal Law, Criminology and Police Science* 52 (November/December 1961):411-417. For a contrary view, see Edward Green, "Inter- and Intra-Racial Crime Relative to Sentencing," *Journal of Criminal Law, Criminology and Police Science* 105 (September 1964):348-358.

2. For example, see Edward F. Bell, "The Black Lawyer and the Judiciary," *Harvard Law School Bulletin* 22 (February 1971):31-35.

3. James Q. Wilson, *Negro Politics: The Search for Leadership* (Glencoe, Ill.: The Free Press, 1960), pp. 256-257.

4. Bruce McM. Wright, "A Black Brood on Black Judges," *Judicature* 57 (June/July 1973):360-365.

5. Roosevelt Johnson, "Black Administrators and Higher Education," in *Black Political Life in the United States,* ed. Lenneal Henderson (San Francisco: Chandler Publishing Company, 1972), pp. 200-214.

Appendix A
Sentence Severity Scale

Scale Value	Number of Cases	Disposition
1	1,746	Suspended sentence
2	201	Fine: $50 or less
3	316	Fine: $51-$100
4	205	Fine: $101-$500
5	6	Fine: $501-$1,000
6	2	Fine: $1,001+
7	124	Suspended sentence plus fine: $50 or less
8	216	Suspended sentence plus fine: $51-$100
9	174	Suspended sentence plus fine: $101-$500
10	9	Suspended sentence plus fine: $501-$1,000
11	3	Suspended sentence plus fine: $1,001+
12	184	Probation: less than 1 year
13	57	Probation: less than 1 year plus fine
14	4,136	Probation: 1 year
15	596	Probation: 1 year plus fine
16	4,275	Probation: 2 years
17	606	Probation: 2 years plus fine
18	3,551	Probation: 3 years
19	496	Probation: 3 years plus fine
20	481	Probation: 4 years
21	49	Probation: 4 years plus fine
22	2,572	Probation: 5 years
23	239	Probation: 5 years plus fine
24	85	Probation: 6 years
25	9	Probation: 6 years plus fine
26	167	Probation: 7 years
27	11	Probation: 7 years plus fine
28	56	Probation: 8 years
29	4	Probation: 8 years plus fine
30	358	Probation: 9 years
31	28	Probation: 9 years or more plus fine
32	1,260	Minimum less than 6 months; maximum 1 year or less
33	149	0 to 11 months—flat
34	5,719	Minimum less than 1 year: maximum 2 years or less
35	236	Minimum 1 year or less: maximum not over 2
36	439	Minimum 1 year or less: maximum not over 3
37	77	Minimum 1 year or less: maximum not over 4
38	204	Minimum 1 year or less: maximum not over 5
39	27	Minimum 1 year or less: maximum not over 6
40	10	Minimum 1 year or less: maximum not over 7
41	5	Minimum 1 year or less: maximum not over 8
42	0	Minimum 1 year or less: maximum not over 9
43	48	Minimum 1 year or less: maximum not over 10
44	13	11 months to 2 years—flat
45	459	Minimum 1-2 years, maximum not over 3
46	84	Minimum 1-2 years, maximum not over 4
47	561	Minimum 1-2 years, maximum not over 5
48	41	Minimum 1-2 years, maximum not over 6
49	85	Minimum 1-2 years, maximum not over 7

Scale Value	Number of Cases	Disposition
50	30	Minimum 1-2 years, maximum not over 8
51	3	Minimum 1-2 years, maximum not over 9
52	180	Minimum 1-2 years, maximum not over 10
53	22	Minimum 1-2 years, maximum not over 20
54	4	2-3 years—flat
55	58	Minimum 2-3 years, maximum not over 4
56	281	Minimum 2-3 years, maximum not over 5
57	39	Minimum 2-3 years, maximum not over 6
58	88	Minimum 2-3 years, maximum not over 7
59	45	Minimum 2-3 years, maximum not over 8
60	2	Minimum 2-3 years, maximum not over 9
61	280	Minimum 2-3 years, maximum not over 10
62	37	Minimum 2-3 years, maximum 10 to 20
63	6	Minimum 2-3 years, maximum not over 20
64	2	3-4 years—flat
65	31	Minimum 3-4 years, maximum not over 6
66	58	Minimum 3-4 years, maximum not over 7
67	23	Minimum 3-4 years, maximum not over 8
68	9	Minimum 3-4 years, maximum not over 9
69	204	Minimum 3-4 years, maximum not over 10
70	133	Minimum 3-4 years, maximum 10 to 20
71	12	Maximum 3-4 years, maximum not over 20
72	2	4-5 years—flat
73	6	Minimum 4-5 years, maximum not over 8
74	1	Minimum 4-5 years, maximum not over 9
75	62	Minimum 4-5 years, maximum not over 10
76	86	Minimum 4-5 years, maximum not over 20
77	9	Minimum 4-5 years, maximum over 20
78	4	5-6 years—flat
79	85	Minimum 5-6 years, maximum not over 10
80	91	Minimum 5-6 years, maximum not over 15
81	53	Minimum 5-6 years, maximum not over 20
82	22	Minimum 5-6 years, maximum over 20
83	14	Minimum 6-7 years, maximum not over 12
84	36	Minimum 6-7 years, maximum not over 20
85	16	Minimum 6-7 years, maximum over 20
86	0	Minimum 7-8 years, maximum not over 14
87	46	Minimum 7-8 years, maximum over 14
88	5	Minimum 8-9 years, maximum not over 16
89	28	Minimum 8-9 years, maximum over 16
90	1	Minimum 9-10 years, maximum not over 18
91	12	Minimum 9-10 years, maximum over 18
92	100	Minimum over 10 years, maximum over 20
93	126	Life imprisonment

Appendix B
An Operational Race-Sentencing Path Model—Simple Correlations (r) (N = 32,731)

	Sentence	Race	Bail Dollars	Bail Status	Number of Charges	Charge Severity	Charge Reduction	Plea	Counsel
Sentence	–								
Race	.16[a]	–							
Bail dollars	.35	.05	–						
Bail status	.46	.17	.23	–					
Number of charges	.24	–.01	.15	.11	–				
Charge severity	.54	.08	.25	.29	.14	–			
Charge reduction	.15	.00	.03	.09	–.06	.47	–		
Plea	.05	.05	–.01	–.02	–.04	–.04	.00	–	
Counsel	–.02	.15	–.06	.23	–.08	–.06	.02	–.05	–

[a]All correlation coefficients larger than .00 are statistically significant at .01 level.

Index

Index

Affirmative action, 3-4
American Bar Association, 7, 55
Americans for Democratic Action, 32
Anti-Ku Klux Klan Act of 1871, 12
Appellate judges, 18, 48, 60n
Association of American Law Schools, 4

Baron, Harold M., 17
Bell, Derrick, 13
Black attorneys, generally, 2-3, 58; community activities of, 16, 55; contributions of, 9, 15; government employment of, 16, 51-52; political involvement of, 16, 55; practices of, 7, 11, 16, 21n, 53
Black attorneys, Metro City, 46; bar examination success of, 46-47; careers of, 47; history of, 46; problems faced by, 47; and white law firms, 47
Black community, 7, 15-16, 58, 102; black attorneys in, 7, 9, 16, 55; black judges in, 11, 63, 105, 108; and economic disadvantage, 7
Black defendants, generally, 1, 14; importance of black judges to, 11; and prior record, 41-42, 83; and race of the victim, 102; representation by black attorneys, 9; representation by public defenders, 19; treatment of, 1, 18-19, 42, 73, 77-78, 83-85, 96n, 102-103, 108
Black defendants, Metro City: sentencing by black/white judges, 18, 66-67, 70-71, 73; treatment of, 18-19, 68, 78-81, 83, 88-91, 93-95, 101
Black elites, 75n; decision making of, 17-18, 63-64, 72, 74, 107; limited power of, 17, 56, 106-107; "traditional" and "second-generation," 73-74, 107-108

Black judges, generally, 1, 2; attitudes of, 10, 18, 25n, 58, 106, 108; backgrounds and careers of, 1, 10, 15-16, 18, 45-46, 53; civil rights activities of, 16, 55; community influences on, 74, 105, 108; contributions of, 9, 11, 15, 23n, 63, 74, 103; decision making of, 17-18, 63, 72, 74-75, 107-108; location of judgeships, 4; representativeness of, 16, 45, 106; research about, 59n, 107-108; roles of, 10-11, 18, 63, 74-75, 103, 105; selection of, 7-8, 16-18, 51, 56; significance of, 13, 17
Black judges, Metro City, 15, 42, 57-58, 74; background and careers of, 16, 51-53, 60n, 63, 106; community influences on, 105-106, 108; decision making of, 18, 64-67, 69, 71-74, 106-107; educations of, 16, 48-51, 60n; interactions with white judges, 104; localism of, 48, 59n, 60n; prior political activity and affiliations of, 53-55, 61n, 107; professional and community activities of, 55-56, 61n, 104-105; representativeness of, 58, 74, 106-107; roles of, 103-104; selection of, 16, 49, 51, 54-57, 106; sentencing of black/white defendants by, 64-67, 69-70
Black law firms, 7, 53
Black legal underrepresentation, 1-2, 8, 12, 15; in bar associations, 3, 7; on the bench, 2-4, 8, 16, 45, 58, 60n; causes of, 4-8, 16-17, 46-47, 49, 50-51; historically, 3, 5, 46; in law school, 2-3, 5-6, 48-50; in private practice, 2-3; in white law firms, 7
Bar examinations, the black experience with, 7, 46-47

Brown v. *Board of Education*, 63
Bullock, Henry Allen, 78
Bylew v. *U.S.*, 12

Canon, Bradley C., 48
Case characteristics, 77, 87-88
Civil Rights Acts of 1866 and 1875, 12
The Civil Rights Cases, 13
Civil War, 12-13
Computerized court data, 37-39
Cook, Beverly Blair, 4
Council on Legal Education Opportunity, 4-5
Crime severity, 38-39, 66-67, 69, 75n, 82-83, 89-90
Criminal courts: and bail practices, 10, 35, 73, 84, 88-90, 93, 102; case disposition in, 19, 34, 82, 88-89, 95; and class-based inequities, 14, 19, 83-85, 88-91, 93; and counsel, 7, 14, 19, 73, 84, 88-89, 91, 93, 101; and plea bargaining, 84, 91; as political institutions, 19-20, 54-55; problems facing, 10, 14, 20; and prosecutors, 14; race issues in, 20, 82, 95, 108; reform of, 14; research on, 101-102, 108
Crockett, George W., 8, 10, 20, 106

Deposit bail, 35
Descriptive representation, 16, 58, 74, 107
Detroit Recorders' Court, 8
Douglass, Frederick, 13, 77

Early case screening, 34-35
Enforcement Act of 1870, 12
Equal opportunity, 63-64, 108
Evans, Robert L., 11

Federal Bureau of Investigation, 30
Fifteenth Amendment, 12
Fourteenth Amendment, 12

Gellhorn, Ernest, 5
Glick, Henry, 53

Glueck, Eleanor, 18
Glueck, Sheldon, 18
Goldman, Sheldon, 49, 53
Green, Edward, 82-83

Harvard Law School, 2
Henderson, Bancroft C., 55
Higgenbotham, A. Leon, 10
Howard, Joseph C., 9
Howard University School of Law, 2, 46

Jackson, Maynard, 6
Jacob, Herbert, 57
Jim Crow laws, 1, 13
Johnson, Roosevelt, 106
Judges, generally: backgrounds and careers of, 51, 53, 60n; background research on, 45-46; community influences on, 38, 74, 103; decision making of, 17-18, 64; education of, 50; localism of, 47-48; recruitment of, 7-8, 51, 53-55, 57-58; socialization of, 18, 38, 63, 74, 106
Judicial autobiographies, 36, 42, 45, 57, 61n
Judicial interviews, 36-37, 57, 65, 103
Justice, 41, 63-64, 74, 77, 107-108

Law: and due process, 10, 107; and its political utility, 14
Law School Admission Test, 5
Law Schools: admissions practices of, 5; black experience in, 6; black law professors in, 6; curricula in, 6; enrollments in, 2-3; historically, 2-3; predominantly black, 6, 48
Legal services, 3

McGovern, George, 28
Metro City, 41: bar association of, 32; blacks in, 27-29; black political leadership in, 29, 107; black political participation in, 28-29, 56, 107-108; crime and clearance rates in, 30, 33-34; criminal justice system in, 30-31, 33-35, 42n, 85, 95, 102-

Index

103; demographics of, 27-29; politics in, 27-29, 54, 56-57
Metro City trial court: anonymity of, 26n, 37, 42n; case disposition in, 34-35, 39-41, 83, 89-91, 102-103; discrimination in, 2, 67, 77, 81, 83, 85, 91, 94-95, 101-103, 108; judge's discretion in, 41, 103; "judge shopping" in, 38; political nature of, 32-33; problems facing, 20, 33-35, 38; race-related versus individual judicial differences, 68, 70-72, 74; recruitment of judges in, 17, 32, 54, 57; reforms in, 33-35, 104; sentencing records from, 37-39, 42, 75n, 100n, 101; similarity to other courts, 35-36, 41; structure of, 31-32, 102, 104
Minority group representation, 16, 45, 56, 58, 74
Montgomery, James, 9
Multiple-charge cases, 39
Myrdal, Gunnar, 1, 9

No-fault automobile insurance laws, 7
No-fault divorce laws, 7
Nagel, Stuart S., 18, 63, 84
National Bar Association, 11, 55, 107

Parenti, Michael, 17
Path analysis, 19, 77, 82, 86-88, 92, 97n, 98n, 99n, 100n, 102, 113
Peterson, Paul E., 64
Pitkin, Hanna, 64
Plessy v. *Ferguson*, 13
Preindictment probation, 35, 102
President's Crime Commission, 14
Prior record, 4, 42, 73, 83, 87, 94-95, 100n, 102
Punishment, purposes of, 41

Race: and criminality, 13, 19, 82-83, 89, 93-94, 96n; and the death penalty, 85; and economic disadvantage, 6-7, 10-11, 13-14, 19, 83, 85, 89, 93; and educational inequities, 4, 21n, 48-50; and negative stereotypes, 7, 10-11, 13-14, 17, 63, 84, 102; and population change, 27, 48
Racial discrimination, 1, 15; alternative explanations for, 82, 85-89, 91, 93-94, 102; in bar examinations, 7, 46; in courts, 1, 8, 10, 12-14, 19-20, 51, 66, 73, 77-78, 83-85, 91, 94-95, 102-103; historically, 1, 12; in judicial recruitment, 8; in law schools, 5, 46, 49-50; in legal associations, 7, 8; in legal hiring, 7
Reidel, Marc, 85
Release-on-recognizance, 35
Reverse discrimination, 73-74

Schlesinger, Joseph, 51
Schmidhauser, John R., 50
Scott, Dred, 12
Semiretired judges, 36, 38
Sentence severity scale, 40-41, 43n, 69, 111-112
Shuman, Jerome, 6, 58
Sinclair, T.C., 55
Slavery, 12
Substantive representation, 16, 64, 74, 107
Supreme Court, U.S., 12

"Tokenism," 2-3, 6-7

Uniform Crime Report, 39

Vines, Kenneth N., 53
Visiting judges, 36, 38, 42n

White-collar crime, 13
White defendants, 2
White judges, 2; interactions with black judges, 10-11, 104; sentencing of black/white defendants by, 64-67, 70
Wilson, James Q., 106
Wolfgang, Marvin E., 85
Wright, Bruce McM., 106

About the Author

Thomas M. Uhlman received his undergraduate degree in political science from the University of Rochester. His M.A. and Ph.D. degrees are from the University of North Carolina at Chapel Hill. Currently an assistant professor of political science at the University of Missouri-St. Louis, Uhlman's articles have appeared in the *American Journal of Political Science, Social Science Quarterly, Western Political Quarterly,* and other social science journals. He is the 1976 recipient of the Edward S. Corwin Award from the American Political Science Association.